William McInnes is one of Australia's most popular writers, delighting readers with his memoirs *A Man's Got to Have a Hobby* and *That'd Be Right*, his novels *Cricket Kings*, *The Laughing Clowns* and *The Birdwatcher*, and his insight into Australian life since the 1940s, written with Essential Media and Entertainment, *The Making of Modern Australia*. In 2011, with his wife Sarah Watt he co-wrote *Worse Things Happen at Sea*, which was named the best non-fiction title in the ABIA and the Indie Awards in 2012.

Also an award-winning actor, William has won two Logies and an AFI Award for Best Actor for his role in the film *Unfinished Sky*. He received critical and public acclaim for his leading role in the film *Look Both Ways*, written and directed by Sarah Watt, and recently starred in the ABC television series *The Time of Our Lives* and *Hello Birdie*.

William McInnes grew up in Queensland and lives in Melbourne with his two children.

Holidays

William McInnes

hachette
AUSTRALIA

These are my own memories of holidays. The names of some people have been changed so that they too can preserve their own memories, in their own ways.

William McInnes

Published in Australia and New Zealand in 2014
by Hachette Australia
(an imprint of Hachette Australia Pty Limited)
Level 17, 207 Kent Street, Sydney NSW 2000
www.hachette.com.au

10 9 8 7 6 5 4 3 2 1

National Library of Australia
Cataloguing-in-Publication data

McInnes, William, 1963– author.

Holidays/William McInnes.

ISBN 978 0 7336 3312 6 (paperback)

Holidays – Australia – Anecdotes.
Vacations – Australia – Anecdotes.
Holidays – Planning.
Reminiscing.
National characteristics, Australian.

394.30994

Cover design by Christabella Designs
Cover photograph of William McInnes taken by Sarah Watt
Back cover photographs from the family albums of Christa Moffitt
Inside front cover: Stella McInnes; inside back cover: Colin and Iris McInnes. All photographed by Sarah Watt, courtesy of William McInnes
Text design by Bookhouse, Sydney
Typeset in Bembo
Printed and bound in Australia by Griffin Press, Adelaide, an Accredited ISO AS/NZS 14001:2009 Environmental Management System printer

To PB, Niall and Leon – three grand friends

Prologue

I once had a part-time clerical job in a public service department that dealt with family allowance forms. We were given the rather unfortunate title of FA Monitors, or Sweet FA monitors, as one man, George, insisted on saying when he answered the phone.

'That's all we do, sweet FA,' he said with a smile.

I couldn't really disagree; we all seemed to simply sift through our forms, stamp a section and file them away in large yellow envelopes that then disappeared down to a room in the basement. Although the work was dull, the Sweet FA monitors were an interesting group of people.

George, a bearded man with round rimless spectacles, was a Christian Brothers old boy who looked like an illustration from an 1890s Anarchist International handbook, which was apt as he happened to be a member of the International Socialists.

There was a Polish vet who was waiting for her academic credentials to be recognised in Australia, and a large woman who put sugar on her hot chips because she was diabetic. I only found this out when I asked her why she was pouring the contents of a large plastic Saxa salt container over her fried food.

'Sugar,' she corrected.

'Sorry?' I said.

'It's sugar.'

'Sugar.' I nodded.

'Because I am diabetic,' she said.

I didn't know if that made any sense but I nodded again.

'Why do you put the sugar in the salt container?'

'Because it makes me feel normal.'

'Nobody puts that much salt on their chips,' George said.

'It's sugar.'

'You are normal,' a woman who looked like Oscar Wilde said.

'Am I?' said the sugar salt sprinkler.

'You are to me,' said Oscar Wilde. 'Very normal.'

'Thank you.' And she sprinkled more sugar from the salt container.

One of the Sweet FA monitors was a strange man who hardly said anything but had a habit of whistling Kiss's 'I Was Made For Loving You' as he walked through the office. He was a small, emaciated man with lank hair and a drooping moustache who reminded me of Mathew Brady photographs from the American Civil War. He floated through the halls like the spectre of one of General Grant's whiskey-swilling inner circle.

Our supervisor, Don, was anything but a spectre: a stocky man with a surfer's bleached shoulder-length hair, tight pants and short-sleeved shirts always adorned with a broad tie.

He had rather bad skin and would walk about with a nod, dipping a finger in his mouth and then daubing a bit of spittle on something he was picking at on his arm.

Once a day, the world's most violent tea lady would storm about and bully people into buying something from her trolley, all the while dispensing personal advice and character assessments.

'You want to put a bit more weight on, mate,' she said to the Civil War spectre.

'Still picking at yourself, Don? Feed your hobby with some choccy! Zit fertiliser.'

Don smiled as he bought some chocolate and picked at himself.

The section manager was a man called Kerry, with a Dennis Lillee moustache and neatly combed, tortured hair. He was either constantly on the phone or going through calculations in a low mutter at his desk.

It was only when I was moved closer to Kerry's desk and overheard his conversations that I started to understand how far and wide the FA monitors' work spread.

Kerry spoke like a radio presenter from 4IP during Rock-tober, smooth and certain, save for the fact he couldn't pronounce his r's. Which was slightly unfortunate, seeing as his name was Kerry. Or Ke-wee, as he pronounced it.

'Okay, Slacks Cweek are all in and the Northern suburbs are done. Gweat.' A few phone calls later, 'Amewica, West Coast and Wocky Mountains?' and then, 'What about a Bawwier Weef for the short term?'

From Slacks Creek to the Rocky Mountains to the Great Barrier Reef.

I was never sure what any of us was supposed to be doing but, in between creating a ball made of discarded rubber bands the size of a soccer ball and stamping my forms, the most exotic suburb that I saw mentioned on any form was Lota, down past Wynnum but nowhere near the Rockies.

On my final day, during a tea trolley round, Kerry enlightened me as to what we Sweet FAs did.

I asked the tea lady for a Cherry Ripe, Don picked at himself, the Polish vet bought an apple, and the sugar salt sprinkler asked for a couple of salt sachets to mix up her chip seasoning. Oscar Wilde sat smiling. The tea lady asked me how my last day was going.

'No last-day shivers, Stretch? Not worried about where you're going?'

I told her I was okay and that I never really knew what it was we were doing there anyway.

There was a silence.

Eventually Rock-tober Kerry filled it.

'Intwesting, Willyum. Intwesting. Not just about forms and filing what we do here, you know. Just a means to an end. We pwovide a service, twue, but it's a means to an end.'

'To what?'

Rock-tober Kerry laughed. 'To what? I'm fairly incwedulous, Will. To *what?*'

It was like I was some poor sod who had missed a basic truth about the purpose of work.

There was a gurgle behind me from the Civil War spectre. I looked at him and realised to my astonishment that he was talking.

'Holidays,' he said, smiling.

Everyone else around the trolley nodded. 'Holidays.' And they laughed.

I understood.

Holidays.

'How you measure your good times,' said Kerry. He winked at the tea lady. 'Will's Chewee Wipe is on me.'

It was as if a life could have its happiness measured in holidays.

Work and toil might be a part of life, even at the Sweet FAs, but it is the golden moments of a holiday – with your children, your partner, your loved ones and friends – that you remember. They can determine your happiness.

I like to think all the Sweet FAs had holidays they remembered.

Because for them, like so many Australians, a holiday is a special time that you have either worked hard and long for, or come by with a stroke of good luck, or simply look forward to achieving. It's a reward for lasting through work or school, or some period of life, to reach that state of nirvana of being on holiday.

But first, before that blissful state, you have to understand what a holiday actually is and then perhaps you'll understand what it means to you.

The First Holiday

The first holiday I can remember going on was with my mother and brother and three sisters. We waved goodbye to the dog, a rusty red Kelpie cross called Michael, and my father, who was called Colin by my mother and Col by every other person we or he ever came into contact with.

Col and Michael stood at the gate as we rolled away on the green Hornibrook bus that would take us across a long and bumpy bridge to Sandgate railway station. We were to board a train to South Brisbane, then another to Sydney and another to Camden, west of Sydney, where we were to stay with my aunt on a dairy farm.

Train travel meant going to Brisbane, I was only six but I knew that much. That meant the Brisbane Show or a movie or the museum, with the German tank and the dinosaur outside. Or lunch in the Coles cafeteria with the ladies in the white uniforms and the crumbed sausages with yellow runny cheese in the middle, and roast chicken and gravy. Gravy without lumps, almost unimaginable.

At home, Mum would have a crack at gravy and my father would say, 'You've mined the harbour again, 'Ris!' as he happily sifted through the little balls of flour in Mum's gravy.

'Well, try cooking for you lot,' my mother would say.

A holiday could also mean plastic cups of lime jelly with cream and a chocolate frog.

But this train trip holiday was special because we were not only going to Brisbane but past Brisbane. I had no concept of what was past Brisbane but my eldest sister, Laurie, explained the holiday to me.

'We're going on a trip. A long trip. A long, *long* train trip.'

She might as well have said that we were sailing round the world but she assured me that it would be worth it.

At Sandgate railway station, the holiday began.

We waited, teetering on the edge of the platform to watch for the approaching train until we were grabbed and hauled back by our mother's hand.

After the train arrived, we scrambled on board and peered out the windows. From the top carriage, we scanned the backyards that slowly rolled past and counted the number of above-ground pools.

It was exciting. Especially as my sister Corby had told me that we might see proper pools. In-ground pools. I looked into backyards filled with fibro sheds, banana trees, cars on blocks and caravans.

I spotted an old dog barking and an old woman with a cane yelling at an old man who looked away and waved his arm at her.

'Are they on holiday?' I asked.

My mother laughed.

I saw a little girl standing still beneath a Hills Hoist holding on to a towel and staring out at the train.

'She's not going on a holiday,' said one of my sisters.

I waved as we chugged slowly past the girl. She kept holding the towel, but with her other hand she gave a slight, slow wave.

But I never saw any proper pools.

When we arrived at far distant South Brisbane I was stunned to discover that we weren't in Camden yet.

I still wasn't clear on what a holiday was, despite my mother explaining to me earlier in the week that a holiday is a bit of time where you do lovely things that you otherwise never get the chance to ever really do.

Like?

My sister Corby went to the *Oxford Dictionary*, which I knew would explain what a holiday was, for there was no word that it did not explain. The worth of this book was proven when my elder sisters would take great delight in telling me the definition of fart – 'an emission of pungent gas/wind from between the legs'.

It was, I think, the funniest thing anyone had ever read out from a book, barring the time my father had attempted to read a story to me in bed without his glasses. He couldn't see a word of the book about the three little pigs so he decided to make it up.

Dad stood up for the wolf because 'Old Wolfie' did what wolves were supposed to do and never complained. Wolfie seemed to take his fate like a man, or, as my father put it, 'Copped it fair on the chin without a whimper', even when he fell in the pot of boiling water. The pigs, on the other hand, were all soft, podgy and had tickets on themselves.

Particularly the pig from the house of bricks. For some reason Dad had it in for this pig. 'Smug, fat little sod, that's what he is,' muttered my dad. 'Where'd he get the money to pay for that? Eh?'

My father had it sorted; Old Wolfie hadn't fallen into a boiling pot of water but had jumped into a bath. The fat little pig who hid in his house of bricks hadn't given Wolfie any soap for the bath and so, quite reasonably, Wolfie jumped out of the water, gobbled up the pigs and then opened up a pub that sold sarsaparilla.

The three little pigs would forever be coloured by that evening's night-night read.

But when it came to holidays, the *Oxford Dictionary* gave only a rather dry and befuddling definition. Maybe if my father could have read it without his glasses it might have been better, but he was out working.

I had to make do with this: 'holiday – an extended period of leisure and recreation, especially one spent away from home or travelling'.

Leisure and recreation were explained as things like reading, running, swimming, playing, relaxing and watching telly.

These were things I spent most of my time doing. So I still didn't quite know what a holiday was because, really, all my life had seemed a holiday.

But I knew this thing called a holiday was different, because we all got dressed up for it.

I cried because my mother had the final say on what was suitable and I couldn't wear an ice-cream bucket as a helmet.

And because I wasn't allowed to wear a t-shirt.

The button-up shirt was what my mother wanted; I had to look like I belonged to someone. It was special. We were going on holidays.

So for the next sixteen hours on the train we wore our best clothes.

'It's important to let people know that we've made an effort,' Mum said.

A holiday was also important enough to pack food for. Not as in food for a picnic or day trip but a bag with platoons of sweet corn sandwiches, a battalion of boiled eggs, and tubes of condensed milk with a polar bear on the side.

We ate on the train and bits of corn spilled here and there, and rolled around the carriages. My brother, Vaughan, put some corn in his mouth and smiled as if he had only a few old yellow teeth in his head. 'Kissy on ya yips! Kissy on ya yips,' he said to me.

I squirmed and wriggled, whined and lost the contents of my sweet corn sandwich over my good shorts.

Vaughan laughed and puckered his lips, and his yellow sweet corn teeth spilled out onto the floor.

My mother shook me and gave Vaughan a flick. 'Stupid boys.'

I wondered if this was her leisure time, sitting with her tribe of unruly children. Even though it must have been like wrangling cats in a bag, she looked sort of happy. It was a holiday.

A holiday in a train carriage for hours and hours as we trundled past small towns. Our copious boiled eggs ensured that the carriage was filled with a fair amount of pungent gas being emitted from between the legs. Thanks to the *Oxford Dictionary*.

Why my father didn't come on the holiday was a mystery to me.

'Someone's got to work' was the answer I received. I knew Dad left early in the mornings and came home in the early evenings. And I knew that when he was at work he banged things with hammers and sawed things. And when he was at home he would bang things with hammers and saw things.

So I took it to mean that he and Michael the dog were both working at work and working at home.

'Now don't go changing anything without letting me know about it first,' Mum had said as he kissed her goodbye on the cheek.

'You'll be right,' he said and waved.

He actually waved a lot, even before we were gone, almost as if he couldn't wait for us to go so he could have the house to himself.

My mother must have had slightly similar thoughts. 'Not a thing,' she said again and my father had smiled his big smile and waved.

'You'll be right,' he had said. 'Though I don't know why you lot want to get out of Reddy. People come here to holiday, don't you know.'

This was true. When we were home in Redcliffe I could always spot people from out of town.

'People from the country,' my mother would say, as we would watch people in strange clothes, big hats and loud voices.

Then there were countless young kids walking in groups or being chaperoned by a single grown-up. They had loud voices and sometimes had Aboriginal boys and girls with them.

'Bush children,' my mum would say.

There was a place up at Scarborough called the Bush Children's Home that was set right on the water. It was a big house where kids from the bush would come for a holiday.

I stared at an Aboriginal boy outside of Monsignor Brawley's Fun Fair at Scarborough one hot afternoon and he stood aside from the other bush children and stared back at me.

We didn't say anything to each other but he seemed sort of excited to be heading into the fun fair's modest collection of rides and lucky-dip stands.

I couldn't work out why he wore a heavy jumper.

Some older boys, mid teenagers I think, slung about by the pavement had noticed him and his jumper.

'Hey, you bloody boong, how hot are you?' one cried.

'Abo dick,' said another.

The boy's face changed slightly. He didn't seem so excited, he didn't seem so happy. He looked at me, expressionless.

The boys on the pavement laughed and nobody, I think, really cared. I was mystified. What was the joke?

Yes, people came from all over to holiday in Redcliffe.

One night as we were watching telly, my mother told me that one of Nana Mouskouri's guests, a man called Acker Bilk, holidayed in Margate on the Redcliffe Peninsula, of all places. On the telly, he was wearing a bowler hat and an unusual waistcoat, and he had a funny little beard on his chin. As if he'd borrowed it from Colonel Sanders and coloured it in with a black texta.

He played the clarinet and had a song called 'Stranger on the Shore'. My father muttered that if Acker dressed like that in Redcliffe then he certainly wanted to watch himself.

'Why?' said my mother.

'He's what his song says he is, a stranger on the shore. A very strange stranger on the shore.'

The heady mixture of seeing someone on telly, especially someone from Nana Mouskouri's show, and knowing that they holidayed in Redcliffe, confirmed the central importance of the peninsula in terms of holidays.

Perhaps even Nana herself would cross the long and bumpy bridge to enjoy the fare from the fish and chip shop at Scotts Point known to all as 'The Greeks'.

People came to the Redcliffe Peninsula, nobody ever left. Except the Bee Gees, but they were only here on holiday when you really looked hard at it. No, nobody ever left Redcliffe for a holiday.

The local paper, the *Redcliffe Herald*, reinforced this. It came out every Wednesday and was the principal source of news and authority on all things Redcliffe.

The front page was a succession of men from service clubs shaking each other's hands as new office bearers were sworn in. They were almost interchangeable. The Apex with the Rotarians and then on to the Lions.

Occasionally their wives would be granted the honour of having their full names printed alongside those of their husbands.

'It's always the young bloods from Apex that get their wives' names in,' said my mother, as if she had uncovered a conspiracy theory.

The most popular column was entitled 'Through Your Window' and had a graphic of a featureless man watching what was going on inside a house. It was a rather eerily entertaining collection of gossip from around the traps with uncannily obvious attempts to hide the identity of whoever it was who was being gossiped about.

When it came to travel, though, there was little or no content, as if the mere idea was un-Redcliffean. There were mentions of life across the bumpy bridge that led out of the peninsula and of the outside world but these were confined to a few specific, recurring themes.

An old favourite standby was UFO sightings made by residents of Clontarf and Kippa-Ring. Why folks from these two suburbs were more likely to see evidence of extra-terrestrial life in the skies was always puzzling to my father. 'I can make sense of blokes from Clontarf seeing the saucers because they've got the two pubs and the golf club, but Kippa-Ring is dry. And why would you travel all that way across space to have a look at Kippa–bloody–Ring?'

From then on any mention of space travel, UFOs or even science fiction would be linked to Kippa-Ring. Even *Star Wars* was called 'that Kippa-bloody-Ring movie'.

Another glimpse of the outside world occurred when the pages of the *Herald* would have pictures of servicemen in action in the jungles of South-East Asia, as the Vietnam War was still in full swing.

One photo was of Woody Point man Lance Corporal Len Fox on patrol.

Len crouched in the long grass, shadowed by the price list of that week's specials at the Margate Cut Price (baked beans at fifteen cents a can!) and the trots results.

The numbers for the winners' dividends, the prices of the week's specials, and the number of contacts with the Viet Cong were all mixed together in the life of the peninsula.

In another photo two glum-looking soldiers, one from Kippa-Ring and one from Kallangur, stalking off a Pan Am airplane – that international sign of glamorous travel from the movies on the telly – said they considered themselves to be the ultimate island-hoppers. In seven weeks' training with the US Army they had been to five famous Hawaiian Islands.

Hawaii! The place where Elvis made every second movie.

Pan Am, Elvis movie locations, and yet the two soldiers still looked a bit bored. If a holiday did that to Australian diggers, then why would you bother leaving Redcliffe?

In August 1972 there was a photo of a rather nonplussed Graham Yares, an engineering mechanic on HMAS *Teal*, who was sailing off to Papua New Guinea and then the Far East.

If you were attracted to this kind of holiday then below Graham was an advertisement with a dark and shadowy image of a young man with the number twenty plastered over his head, reminding 'young men' to 'register for National Service'.

Well, it could mean a holiday, but my mother hated to be reminded that in a few years her eldest son, Vaughan, might be that shadowy image.

It's not that the *Redcliffe Herald* didn't recognise that the outside world existed – just that it recognised it in its own unique way.

The 23 July 1969 issue mentioned that the moon landing was of great interest to patrons of the Crab Pot Bar at the Ambassador Hotel, almost as if NASA had organised the whole event for the boys at the Crab Pot.

One can hear John F. Kennedy committing America to send men to the moon, 'We choose to send a man to the moon and return him safely to earth not because it is easy but because it is hard and will prove of interest to patrons in the Crab Pot Bar at the Ambassador Hotel!'

The *Herald* had a wonderful way of appropriating the outside world and bringing it home to the peninsula, almost to the point where you could be forgiven for thinking that these foreign places were actually somewhere around the streets and tracks of Redcliffe.

My young mind would be a bit confused when confronted with a huge photo carrying the caption: 'The Grandeur of the Grand Canyon'.

Nestled around the image of a mule train making its way up the twisting trails of the mighty Grand Canyon were the ever-present local trots handicaps and a story about the first amputee trainee in nursing (with the headline 'Lost Leg to Train as Nurse') and, to top it off, a sale at Clem Hoffman's Demolition Yard on Anzac Avenue.

I actually thought for a while that the Grand Canyon might be somewhere round the back of Clem's Yard or somewhere beyond the dump at Clontarf.

If it wasn't the Grand Canyon of Anzac Avenue it was river boats from Mississippi in Bramble Bay and pyramids in Clontarf, always surrounded by the world of the peninsula. There were photos of Redcliffeans returning or recounting tales from holidays, like Miss Sharon Brody, captured returning from her holiday on Hayman Island, which she won for raising the most money in the local Miss Air Force quest.

She looked happy, it was true, but as my father said, 'Why wouldn't she be happy? She's coming back to Reddy.'

It was the same for Mrs C. Praline, who smiled in a high-necked jumper and plaid trousers as she returned to the peninsula for the first time in twenty-seven years. She had married an American serviceman and had made her home in Akron, Ohio, but she was back in Redcliffe on holiday and all she wanted to do, she told the *Herald*, was to eat as much fish and chips and as many dim sims as she could while she was back. 'They don't have anything like that in Ohio,' she said.

It was true; where else could you get crumbed mullet and those boulder-sized, yellow-skinned dim sims but Redcliffe?

Food was a subject through which the *Herald* brought the world to its readers via the 'Cooking Around the World' column by 'Hitch Hiker'.

Want to go to the Balkans? Yes, the Balkans. No need, because 'today's dish comes from the friendly volatile peoples of the Balkans, a mysterious and little-known corner of Europe, perhaps best known for the area called Transylvania'.

The desserts that week came from South America, Mexico and Iceland.

The whole thing was like a gourmet train smash at the United Nations.

Even when somebody from Redcliffe travelled they always had a good sense of perspective on the whole holiday caper. Just like Mr J. Middleton of Scarborough giving his impression of a recent trip to New Zealand. The roads, he said, were fine, though mostly narrow, and seemed to run in all directions, and there were signs everywhere. He also thought that most 'thinking New Zealanders were in favour of becoming an Australian state'.

Nothing like a 'thinking Redcliffean' opinion.

Every Wednesday, the *Herald* would offer a snapshot of what could be achieved by one of our own who had chosen to holiday.

Beneath yet another changing of the Rotary Guard and yet another UFO sighting from Kippa-bloody-Ring was a photo of Barbara Wallace from Redcliffe and her unnamed friend sitting beneath the signpost at Land's End in Great Britain. She had been on a three-year working holiday and on her way back she (and presumably her unnamed friend) were going 'to add spice to their journey by travelling overland by bus and were going to visit Kathmandu, in the Himalayas'.

Barbara was the daughter of Redcliffe's fire chief, a rather dapper-looking Englishman with a neat moustache, who wore a silver helmet.

We used to see him next door in the fire station dressed up in his uniform.

It was strange to think that someone who lived next door to us, like I presumed Barbara did in my small boy's brain, could possibly want to holiday in all these places so far from Redcliffe.

And on a bus too. Did the green Hornibrook bus go that

far? Or was it the Elson's red bus service that took more mysterious routes?

My mother and father were friends of the dapper fire chief with the neat moustache and silver helmet and well-travelled daughter.

'It's not a real holiday, it's a working holiday. She's doing jobs all the time,' they explained to me.

So if you wanted to go on holiday you had to work to justify taking the time away?

'We can't all have fun on holiday, you know, somebody has to keep things going.' Those were my father's last words as he eagerly waved us goodbye.

Transporting five children interstate might have been my father's idea of fun but my mother never said anything. Eventually the train, and us, got to her.

The train was such an important part of that first holiday because it was another world in itself. The dark, winding carriages and compartments that rolled to and fro, and the way we were gently rocked as we walked the aisles to the little shop that sold bits and pieces of chewy and chocolate and bags of crisps. Or we'd walk to the drinking basin that pulled down from the wall with two glasses either side of a glass beaker.

We'd sway past the odd paintings on the walls. A long tall glass of beer advertising Resch's; Namatjira landscapes, one with an Aboriginal man standing with the sole of one foot stuck flat to the knee and shin of his other leg. A spear held upright.

Right beside the water basin.

'He's standing there waiting for a drink!' one of the railway stewards said. 'Always just standing there, watching you drink!' Those stewards were all so immense, seeming too big for the carriage, with large noses and short, oiled hair and loud crackling voices.

And one, louder than the rest, louder even than the creaking train, had a jaw that sawed from side to side when he spoke, as if it was slightly unhinged. He was a bit like Bill the Steam Shovel off the *Mr Squiggle* show.

Mr Squiggle was an odd, stuttering puppet with curly hair, freckles and a pencil for a nose that miraculously could make a discernible picture from a scribble sent by some kid somewhere in Australia.

And Bill was a loud, sleepy-eyed steam shovel with a blaring, broad voice.

The steward had Bill's voice.

For hours we kids roamed up and down the train and my mother never said anything until the toilet. She had managed her wild tribe of children and the sweet corn and eggs but it was the toilet that did it, and me.

The toilet was a tight cold cupboard where barely one person could fit in to do their business. But the size was not the toilet's true terror.

'Just wait till you go to the toilet and do number twos.' My brother smiled.

I stared.

He smiled.

'Mum, what's wrong with the toily?'

My mother said there was nothing wrong with the toilet.

'Just you wait,' said my brother.

I had to go sooner or later and when I did – wanting to make sure that there wasn't substance to my brother's teasing – I whined until one of my sisters came with me.

Corby and I rocked towards the toilet. When we passed the painting of the Aboriginal man with his spear, Corby told me, 'I'm not going in there with you, you know. You're a big boy now.'

She assured me she'd be outside. I opened the stiff, hard little door and closed it. I stood in the cupboard and stared down at the stainless-steel toilet.

It didn't look threatening at all. Just another toilet. Vaughan was only teasing.

'Hurry up,' said Corby from outside the door.

I got down to business and lifted the lid. And screamed.

Below the toilet was a blur, like someone flicking through the pages of a picture book quickly. The strange funnel-shaped bowl was like a crazy kaleidoscope giving a distorting view of what whizzed by below. I suddenly saw the sleepers of the train tracks sliding past like giant piano keys.

And the noise was like some great roaring monster. I wasn't going to use that toilet. There wasn't any need.

I did what I had to do in my pants. I knew one thing – I didn't want to do a number two down the cupboard's roaring hole.

My mother took charge of the trips to the toilet after that.

The next time I had to go, my mother assured me that I wouldn't fall through because nobody ever had. I nodded and she kissed my head and said she would wait outside.

My brother smiled and said, 'Don't fall through!'

My mother flicked a hand at my brother and pushed me along the rocking carriage.

She patted me on the head and I felt like a Christian heading off into a Coliseum full of roaring lions.

I lifted the lid, the hole roared, I screamed and my mother yelled. It was a ritual we enacted over and over again.

She would hold me, squirming in her great strong arms, yelling at me, 'Stop wriggling about! Just sit there and do it.'

I clung to her in the cupboard, because I knew she wouldn't let the roaring hole take me. When I had done what I had to do I leapt off like I'd been electrocuted and tried to climb up my mother.

'You've got to wipe your bottom, you stupid boy,' said my mother.

It was a little like the James Bond fight in the train carriage, only in a more matricidal manner.

Then my six-year-old brain had a moment of inspiration – perhaps when the train stopped the hole wouldn't roar. I waited until the train stood still at a larger station and I scurried off to the cupboard.

Everything was still, no rocking, no sliding. I lifted the lid. No roar. A silent throne. No blur. Just a single piece of timber below.

I sat and prepared myself. Then I screamed. The cupboard door had been flung open and Bill the Steam Shovel railway steward stood there with his great voice booming from his swinging jaws.

'No use of the toilet when the train is stationary, when the train is stationary!'

I got such a fright that I ran past and forgot to pull my pants up.

My mother hitched up my pants and dragged me back to our seats, past the paintings and posters, and sat me down.

She managed to conquer the toilet in the end but it was only a matter of time before the holiday train got the upper hand.

Some new passengers were on the train. Two of them were a young Italian couple. He was happy and eager. She was young and very pretty and wore beautiful soft clothes.

She sat not far from us and smiled as I passed by with my mother. After a while she looked towards my mother, who quite frankly and justifiably, probably felt like she was having anything but a time of recreation and leisure.

'All yours,' said the young woman in an Italian accent and she nodded to us five children as we draped ourselves over and around the seats.

'All of them,' said my mum.

The young man laughed and put his arm around the young woman and pulled gently at the skin beneath her soft clothes.

'Some day we will have children,' he said.

Her soft eyes looked at all of us. She didn't smile and she looked down.

The couple got off just before Sydney and as the young woman readied herself to leave she gave us children and Mum some sugar-covered almonds and pieces of nougat wedding cake.

As they walked along the platform, we all waved to them and they smiled back.

My mother said quietly as the young woman walked away, 'Poor little thing.'

I had another unsuccessful trip to the roaring cupboard before we changed trains at Sydney for Campbelltown and I still had wet pants as my exhausted mother dragged us to our new train.

'It can only get better, it can only get better,' she whispered like a prayer and then she began to laugh.

Above us at Central Station a huge flock of flying foxes rolled over the sky. We all stared.

'Just look at that,' said my mother, 'that's the way to travel.'

That train to Campbelltown happened to be a steam train and the smell of the smoke was strong.

I said incessantly that I wanted to see the smoke and my mother finally decided, why not? She held me outside the window in her big strong hands.

'Can you see the smoke?' she yelled.

I tried to say yes but got a mouthful of soot and ash. So I nodded.

That was when my first holiday really began, for it's not every day a mother holds her youngest out a train window. In my mother's hands, and hearing her laugh, I knew that this holiday, this train holiday, was fun.

When we drove up the winding track that led to the farm Aunty Rita was managing, and where we were going to stay, it was exciting.

Of the rest of the holiday, I remember flashes, a little like a slide night.

Getting out of the car and smelling the cow shit.

Gumboots lined along the wall of the laundry waiting to be filled with our skinny legs. My aunty called them wellington boots. When I asked what the difference between wellington boots and gumboots was she said that 'people could spend a lifetime trying to find the difference if they wanted but it was best just to put them on and get going'.

Aunty Rita told us to wear one wellington boot and one gumboot just to keep things even. I thought this a marvellous idea and did so.

The laundry had a huge copper boiler that was immense and sullen like some sacrificial altar, which was quite fitting because we had to help pluck and drain a chook for dinner. It was a rooster. The feathers were soft and colourful and the flesh warm and clinging.

On that farm we had to help as much as we could, so perhaps it was a case of a working holiday, like the daughter of the dapper fire chief.

We helped with the milking of the warm, sweet-smelling cows. Some had colds and would stand at the stall and sneeze. As they sneezed great streams of shit would flow from under their tails. We children ran with shovels to catch the poo and carry it to a designated 'soup bowl' in the yard, which was just a hole in the ground.

We would run screaming and laughing and squealing as our one wellington boot and one gumboot would not only be filled with a collection of McInnes skinny pins but also 'cow stream' as my aunt called it.

In the house were musical instruments of all sorts: wind organs, tubas, trumpets, cornets and trombones. With our filled-to-the-brim boots we would make whatever sound we could on the instruments as we paraded around the yard.

The farm was surrounded by what my mother called the Chinese Wood, a collection of trees and thickets that carried the detritus and debris from a flood in its branches – Chinese market gardeners' hats, bits and pieces of clothing and strange little shoes. Somehow my mother made a few bits of rubbish seem like a magical fairy tale.

'If you stay too long in the Chinese Wood you hear the sighing of the poor Chinese because they are working so hard in the gardens.'

And the wind would blow and I'd hold her hand as I heard the Chinese sighs.

We caught a rabbit, which was a joint effort worthy of Eisenhower's efforts in coordinating D-Day, and as we wondered how we could take it back to Redcliffe as a pet it scratched the bejesus out of my sister Corby's legs so my mother booted it away as if it were a Steeden rugby ball.

Near the lower part of the farm were the fields of a monastery and my aunty would look to see if 'the handsome monk' was there; she said this in the tone of somebody searching for some rarity. One day as we were walking she let out a laugh and waved. 'Oh, there he is – the handsome monk!'

A man on a tractor in the fields turned, smiled and waved back.

Whether he was handsome or not nobody could tell, but he was smiling and he waved.

'Oh, I do like the handsome monk,' said Aunty Rita, and chuckled.

The monastery had its own tip and when we went walking down the tracks one afternoon we could see one of the monks throwing out piles of rubbish.

We waited and then ran to see what we might discover in the monk's treasure. We quickly sifted through what was there – pieces of beautiful silken cloth.

'Altar cloth,' said my mother. There were also garments with seeds sewn into them that had been blessed by somebody connected with the Holy Father at a place called the Vatican.

And, for some reason, there were also navy uniforms, pale blue cotton drill shirts and white three-quarter shirts with blue trim, badges with radio operator icons on them and bolts of lightning.

We claimed some and in time the 'altar cloth' found its way onto one of our Christmas trees when my mother fashioned the strips of silk into little Arabic and biblical garments and dressed up some of my plastic toy soldiers as figures from the Nativity.

There was the occasional telephone call from my father and some interrogation from my mother.

'What have you done, Colin?'

She would listen and then ask, 'What do you mean, a surprise?' Then, after she had told him that she loved him too and blown a kiss down the line and hung up, she would mutter, 'What has that bloody man done?'

And then she would laugh with my aunt.

We had a party, and my mum and aunty cried and hugged, and then my aunty hugged and kissed us all and we went to sleep, woke up and left.

Left the Chinese Wood and our wellington and gumboots. We looked but didn't see the handsome monk, waved goodbye to our aunt and boarded a train to catch another train and then another and then another.

Somehow the roaring hole wasn't as scary as the first time I had encountered it and, even though I wasn't entirely comfortable, at least I remembered to wipe my bottom before I leapt off.

Apart from that, the journey home was something I have no discernible memory of, save for coming back from Sandgate station on the green bus over the long and bumpy bridge, getting off at the stop just a way from our home and walking up the drive, hearing Michael bark.

And my father appearing with a big smile and looking rather tentative as my mother's eyes swept the house to see what he had renovated.

Just before she could yell he covered her in a big hug and said, 'Now 'Ris, it'll look smashing when it's finished.'

A wall or a window or door had disappeared.

I knew my first holiday had ended and a part of me couldn't wait for the next one to come along.

School Holidays

It wasn't until my life was given a more regimented set of time measurements at school that the idea of holidays became clearer to me. The most memorable signal of school boundaries was the school bell.

It made no difference that the bell at the beginning and at the end of a school day was rung for the same amount of time and sounded exactly the same – the emotions it elicited and the characteristics attributed to the bell were poles apart.

The morning bell was impatient and sharp while the afternoon bell took its time and, once heard, was never quite believed. It was simply too good to be true. In the morning as soon as the bell rang there was a few seconds of dead silence and then a collective groan as the students thought about what was coming throughout the day.

Then once the arvo bell went off, there was a few seconds of suspicious quiet until the bell was believed and the sigh of relief and release was palpable.

Before that bell came into my life, the days of the week all rolled into each other with a pleasing enough anonymity, made separate perhaps by an odd characteristic that some days would hold, like Wednesday being half shopping day for retailers on the Redcliffe Peninsula and Friday the day we ate fish.

School gave new meaning to the days of the week. Monday became the undeniable beginning; the start of the way ahead. The school bell told me so. Tuesday and Thursday became ports of call for life away from school because that was when sports practice began. Wednesday became midweek 'tune-up day', according to my mum. Trips to the dentist, the doctor and the barber were organised for this day. And Friday – well, Friday was still the day we ate fish but it became, more importantly, the day of the finish line.

There was no sweeter sound than the bell on a Friday afternoon, when my new life of being compartmentalised into terms and then semesters was given a respite. The school bell was interrupted by the sanctuary of the weekend.

Soon these two days that made up the weekend began to fall into the set pattern of my new life.

Saturday was free but usually filled with the general business of doing stuff: sport, idling on the beach or racing to the shops with a parent or elder sibling. Still, there was always another day left in the weekend so it didn't seem too bad. Sunday was the problem.

Things were closed, even petrol stations, and when the highlight of the morning was the pass the ball competition on Channel Seven's *Sportscene* it showed you knew time was floating along.

Unshaven, and usually hung-over, bleary-eyed football players would do their best to pass a ball through the behind of a happily smiling Commonwealth Bank elephant.

If they managed to pop the ball through the arse of the elephant, somebody, probably the cigarette-puffing host Rod Gallegos, would press an air hooter and say, 'No wonder Jumbo is looking happy! Nice one, son.'

Somehow a Sunday afternoon seemed to swim along forever but when it ended you knew the sound of the school bell was what awaited you the next morning.

But the bell giveth and taketh away.

For the bell also gave the signal that a new and wondrous part of my life was beginning. School holidays.

These weren't to be confused with the little isolated islands of delights of the public holiday, which came as a sweet surprise and on the surface were primarily a form of Floating Sundays when everything was shut for everyone. School holidays were different – they belonged to us kids, to do with them what we wanted, or so I thought.

At first the holidays were like elongated weekends so, accordingly, I just buggered around as usual. Then it dawned on me that people I took for granted, like our neighbours across the fence, the Worths, would suddenly disappear.

Reg and Warren were my age and were always there to play with every weekend. And every Saturday their dad, Snowy, would mow the lawn and do the garden and then settle in for the afternoon to listen to the races with his wife, one of the sweetest of people, Pat.

The Worths were fun. Especially when Snowy would be doing the garden after a few Friday night beers and Warren would liven things up a bit by putting a full tin of Pat's Cedel Super Hold hairspray in the incinerator as Snowy was engaged in the weekly rubbish burn.

Being an old army man, Snowy would hit the dirt, and then leap into action, first reaching for his belt and then chasing Warren about the newly mown yard.

But one day, all this changed. The Worths disappeared. Where?

Maybe it was connected to something Reg had told me a few days before about how they were going to be on holiday.

'But you are on holidays,' I'd said.

Reg had shrugged. 'No, we're going away for holidays.'

'Going away?'

He'd nodded. 'Yeah, going away, to Taree.'

I had no idea where Taree was but apparently it was a place to go for a holiday.

My mother had nodded when I'd told her and said that the Worths were off to Gay Taree. People used to say that about

Gay Paree, so I immediately assumed Taree was somewhere near Paris.

Taree is a lovely place if you are looking for a small farming community eight hours down the road in New South Wales, but I had it fixed in my tiny mind that the Worths were off to a place even further from Redcliffe than Camden. France.

When I told my father the Worths were going to France he gave me a look that was the same look he reserved for people he loved, like his sons, or people he thought were complete and utter idiots, like rugby referees and any Liberal cabinet minister from New South Wales. 'What is wrong with your son?' he asked of my mother. 'What is the pie can talking about?'

At times when my father was completely at a loss to understand what I was gabbling about he would graciously relinquish responsibility for his fifth and most incoherent child. And, particularly whenever I annoyed him, ownership and responsibility always returned to my mother.

My mother shook her head and said quickly that the neighbours were off for a holiday.

My father's eyes narrowed. 'Does that mean we have to look after the bird?'

My mother nodded.

'Jesus wept,' muttered my father. 'How much is that going to cost?'

'Oh, be quiet, Colin.'

I didn't really know what he was talking about. It wasn't long after the Worths had vanished that my mother brought over a small birdcage containing a blue budgerigar called Peter.

We'd looked after the Worths' pet budgie before when Snowy and Pat had to go off to a relative's funeral. All had seemed to go along well enough and it didn't seem to cost much of anything.

That was during school term. This was holidays. I would be around. And this time we were to look after Peter while the Worths were driving all the way to Taree, way over there in France. For a while this novelty added something to the holidays. Peter had a little mirror encased in a yellow plastic circle, a little bell and two plastic holders for feed and water.

And a swing to sit on, which was just as well because that is about all he did. Until he fell off.

He fell off the day after the Worths left. And he didn't get up.

I didn't know this until my mother exploded, 'Christ, so soon!'

'Here we go, here we bloody go!' muttered my father.

I went over and saw the prone budgie.

'Just having a kip,' said my father. 'We'll make it comfy for him.' And he proceeded to throw a towel over the small cage.

'Here, take this up to Ken MacCohan's and get some chewing gum or something to keep you busy.'

His big brown hand pressed a ten-cent piece into my tiny palms. These holidays were turning out well.

My father never gave me money to spend anywhere. Not even when he was filling the tank of his truck at his preferred servo, Ken MacCohan's BP on the corner of Duffield Road, which seemed as likely a time as any to give me money to spend.

Fathers always seemed to be happy at service stations, a place where everybody spoke twice as loudly as usual and laughed a lot. A little bit like an old Robin Hood movie.

There Dad could have a chat with Ken MacCohan, a stocky, happy man who'd played fullback in one test for Australia and who used to coach the Redcliffe Dolphins.

And there too, at MacCohan's, was a lolly stand where ten cents went a long way – two packets of Musk Beechies chewing gum. Looking good.

I ordered the two packets as Ken MacCohan and a large man called Tiny yelled and laughed at each other and at the red-haired mechanic covered in grease in the workshop and at some people filling up their cars and at me.

'What's on for you during the holidays, champ?'

I couldn't really think of much other than the budgie.

'We're looking after our neighbours' budgie,' I said.

The men were quiet, glanced at each other and then threw back their heads and Robin Hooded, 'Another one! Well good luck with the budgie, mate!'

I wasn't sure what they meant but I thought perhaps budgies had that effect on people.

I was on my second packet of Beechies when I looked in

on Peter later that afternoon. He seemed to have woken up and was quite energetic.

He leapt from his swing and clung to the bars of the cage and appeared to shriek more than sing. He was also attacking the little mirror quite a lot.

'He seems to be much happier,' said my mother.

He was certainly much faster, almost manic, and also seemed a bit smaller than he had been in the morning.

At night my father glanced up from his dinner as Peter shrieked from his cage.

'Jesus wept,' he whispered into his pile of food.

My mother gave him a stare and he shook his head.

'Well, at least he looks the same,' he muttered.

'Colin!' my mother almost yelled.

Peter shrieked.

My father shrugged.

Peter's little bell rang.

Sometime over the next morning Peter's behaviour seemed to have changed yet again. He was very quiet, with a beach towel draped over his cage.

'He's sleeping,' my mother said curtly.

'No wonder, after all the noise he made last night,' said my father and then he looked over to me. 'Did you have to go and tell Kenny MacCohan about looking after that bird?'

He turned to my mother, 'All they bloody did was ask how the budgie was going as I filled up the truck,' he said, shaking his head. 'Laugh a minute.'

When the towel came off Peter's cage, the change was confirmed: he seemed bigger and much calmer. He didn't move much at all.

Perhaps that was because of what he must have done to his claw.

'What's happened to Peter's leg?'

'His leg?' asked my mother.

'Well . . .' I looked at Peter, who definitely had undergone a life change. Not only was he bigger and calmer, he only had one claw.

My mother came over and looked at the budgie.

'Oh bugger, I didn't see that. That is a giveaway, isn't it? No wonder he's so quiet.'

I stared at my mother and she looked down at me. I could see she was deliberating about something and she decided to take me into a confidence concerning Peter the budgie, a confidence that had been shared with the rest of my family.

'Peter died,' she said.

I thought I should be upset; maybe even attempt to cry a bit.

'Oh, stop that, you're as obvious as that bird's claw. It's very sad, but he's died a number of times.'

'Did we kill the Worths' budgie?'

'No, we didn't. Mean to. It's awful but they're finicky little things and they don't seem to last that long in a cage. I don't know.' She paused.

My father decided to help. 'Everything has to drop off their perch sooner or later.'

'Yes, they seem to do it sooner rather than later, which is a shame.'

It dawned on me that perhaps this wasn't the first time that Peter, or Peters, may not have thrived under our care.

'Did Peter . . . did other Peters go to sleep when we looked after them?'

My mother decided to take me further into her confidence.

'Well of course, that last time they went off to the funeral it was two Peters we went through.'

'Perhaps it's because we're so loud,' said my sister Corby. 'They go into shock.'

My mother sighed. 'Well, that's just the way we are.'

'Won't the Worths know that we killed the budgie?' This time I nearly did cry.

'We don't kill the things. They're finicky.' My mother was loud and quite a force to be reckoned with when she got a head of steam up but at heart she was a gentle woman.

'Oh, poor little sods – it's that bloody Myer Christmas hamper.'

Whenever anything unfortunate or problematic happened in our house, it was blamed on the infamous Christmas of the two Myer Christmas hampers. One December morning a Myer's Christmas hamper turned up, as was the tradition. But later that afternoon another miraculously appeared.

My mother was riddled with guilt but delightedly ripped into the hamper and a bumper Christmas was had by all. But as she'd munched on pickled onions from the second hamper, Mum had said, 'Sooner or later we'll have to pay for this.' She always remembered the year of the double hamper and expected she would have to pay for her good fortune eventually.

Now this situation with Peter – or Peters – was the latest Myer hamper payback.

My mother looked back at the budgie cage. 'Oh, those bloody pickled onions.'

Still, she had a plan, as she always did, for my mother had a unique take on the evolving Peters.

'The poor little sods are a bit like popes. They change slightly, some are fat, some are thin, some have glasses, but they all look the same after a while. They all look like popes.'

I wondered if there had ever been any popes with one leg, but you couldn't really tell because I had never seen any Holy Father doing anything else but sitting or maybe waving. Certainly never running.

'And I think we can get away with this fellow,' added my mum, assessing this latest Peter from different angles in his cage.

Nobody else was terribly sure.

Still, things became the most desperate when my father decided to see his 'mate' Peter Linkley down at the back of the Clontarf industrial estate, past the dump.

'You're going to see that man,' said my mother.

Peter Linkley was like a character from the British police show *The Sweeney*.

This was the show where everybody used to scowl when they spoke and nobody wore clothes that looked clean or ironed. Which was just as well, because every ten minutes there was a fight or a car crash or someone spilling beer over somebody else.

Linkley didn't hang around Redcliffe very long and shonky wasn't a word that would come close to describe the whole aura he emitted in his Sweeney attire and attitude, but he always seemed to be a man of some mystery.

He would hire things from my father's hire service, like sledgehammers and large crowbars, and hardly ever pay for them, instead offering Dad things like watches that would stop working after a couple of weeks or would start telling the time backwards. And then there were the radios that were always in unopened cardboard boxes. When they were opened the radios had strange station numbers on the dial.

'Well, it'll be cheaper than buying another one,' said my father.

That afternoon he returned looking a bit nonplussed. He had a bird. A very pretty bird.

'What did you give for that?' asked my mother.

'Let him have two bolt-cutters for the weekend.'

'Bolt-cutters, Colin?' said my mum, slightly shocked.

'Best not to ask, love.' He shook his head.

'What can we do with that thing?'

'It's a bird.'

'It's not even a bloody budgie.'

'I know that, love.'

There was a pause. He glanced at the bird. 'Maybe we could swap it for a transistor?'

'Colin.'

'Just a thought.'

'We'll just have to stick with that one-legged thing.'

The faith in the budgie popes wasn't strong enough to stop an anxious feeling shrouding the rest of the holidays.

On the Saturday of our neighbours' return, when the cage containing the one-legged Peter was handed back to Mrs Worth, I was so sure the whole conspiracy would be uncovered that I gallantly stood on the back verandah of our home to await the shock and horror of the Worths' reaction.

My mother stayed at the Worths' for a cup of tea and returned satisfied with the results.

'Get the puff of white smoke out the chimney, we've got a new pope,' she said with a thumbs-up gesture.

I couldn't quite believe it but she advised me to never mention the budgie pope to either of the Worth boys, saying only, 'Pat is such a lovely woman.'

Years later, my mother told me that when she handed the cage back to Mrs Worth, this sweet woman had nodded and said, 'Well, you've done well there, Iris, he looks lovely and we've had some shocking Peters. Poor little things. They do come and go.'

How she explained the missing claw of this new incarnation of Peter nobody ever knew. The Worths were certainly good sticks.

As for the bird my father had bartered from Peter Linkley, that was sorted when the Sweeney man popped in to return the bolt-cutters to my father.

'Did the job,' he said, and smiled in his Sweeney scowling way as he handed over the bolt-cutters. He then proceeded to ask if he could, ''Ave dat bird bayck, mate? Bit ov a problem, dat bird.'

In return, another radio in a cardboard box with funny stations on its dial was popped in the back shed. And for quite some time after that last week of the school holidays, whenever my father would fill his truck at the BP on the corner, Ken MacCohan, Tiny and the red-haired mechanic would bellow, 'How's that budgie going?' and throw their heads back in Robin Hood laughter.

•

When the impatient school bell rang on the Monday morning after the pope budgie holidays, it sorted out a few things.

That morning at assembly the headmaster, Mr Stevens, a perennially grumpy and ill-tempered man with a glowering brow and bristling moustache, blared through the microphone that holidays were over and that, 'It's back to work and real life.'

He loved that microphone, and he used it well. My brother and sisters had gone through Humpybong and they used to say how much he yelled. The microphone allowed him to growl and then bellow with a great and pleasing effect.

After a while you could tell when Mr Stevens was about to do this because he would lean back so as not to distort the sound too much.

In fact, any club lounge singer would admire his microphone technique. Never a single muffled word.

Mr Stevens was a strange man to me and my relationship to him, although long-standing, was always the simplest and most basic of headmaster and student relationships. Namely, I had many disciplinary visits to his cool dark room in the heart of the school, where a large photo of the Queen smiled from the wall and everything was arranged neatly on his desk. There I would be punished or dismissed to the kindly Mr MacNab to be dealt with.

Years later, as an adult – and working 'at real life' as Mr Stevens would have it – I came across his granddaughter.

She was kind and gentle, and a very valued colleague, and I couldn't quite believe that she was related to this microphone-loving, cane-wielding headmaster.

She told me how much she had loved her pop, and I felt rather awkward at how my memories tallied – or failed to tally – with hers, but I thought that perhaps when he was on holidays he might have been a different man.

It seemed hard to believe, though. She said that in the time just before he died, he believed himself to be the governor-general of Australia and in constant contact with Her Majesty the Queen.

She thought it sweet.

I thought of all the times he had caned me in that dark room with the Queen smirking down at me from the wall. His Queen.

If you imagined you were somebody else at the end of your days, why choose the governor-general? All fluff and no real responsibility; people bowing and doffing their hats to you, not because of who you are but what or whom you represent.

After assembly we went to our classrooms, stood at our desks and then sat.

Real life. And the first task was written composition. 'My Holidays' was the title of the exercise.

In our grey-covered exercise books that seemed to have come from the days of the Depression, with the Queensland crest on the cover and traffic safety illustrations on the back, we were to write about our holidays.

Back in the real life of the schoolroom I didn't have much to tell. I glanced around and saw that others had the same distant look on their faces.

Nobody much else had gone away for the holidays, except for a few day trips. I didn't count the girl with red hair who always came back with a badge bought from some new town her Nanna and Pop had visited. Instead of a suitcase dotted with stickers from exotic locations, she had a cardigan covered with the names of destinations that even I knew were close to Redcliffe.

Kallangur was the most exotic so I knew she could be discounted.

But I was gripped with a worry – what could I write about?

'On my holidays my neighbours went to Taree in France and we looked after their budgie, Peter, that went asleep and fell off his perch and never got back up and then turned into a screaming crazy pretend Peter and then a sloth with one leg. My father tried to get a bird from the Sweeney man but it wasn't right and instead it turned into a weird radio. But in the end it was okay because the budgies are like the Holy Father – even if there is a leg missing.'

I didn't think that would be a good idea.

I sat stupefied. Then I noticed that Bradley Phie was writing easily and quickly. And David Smythe was hard at it too.

Why, I didn't know. I knew these boys went to fewer places than me, even though I knew one had gone to Ipswich to visit a grandparent. Technically I didn't think that counted. I thought about madly appropriating the Worths' trip but outside of Taree being in France I had no idea of what had gone on.

I looked to Bradley Phie and David Smythe again and saw they shared a ruler between them and both were looking at the markings on the ruler and then hurriedly scribbling down their written expression.

A broad wooden ruler with pictures of tourist attractions that could be found in Canberra. Parliament House, the Australian Academy of Science, Lake Burley Griffin and a green field with men in white uniforms called Duntroon.

The ruler was flicked down to me and then flicked back and offered again but this time the owner of the ruler held it just out of my grasp. Bradley Phie lifted his book and showed me his work.

'My Holiday. We went to Canberra and we saw the lake and the parliament house and treasury house.'

They were working their way through the photos on the ruler.

A note then appeared from under Bradley Phie's hand. 'Two cents for the ruler.'

I suddenly understood and nodded; two cents and you have your holiday in your hands to write about.

The ruler got through as many hands as it could, giving us the ingredients to make what we could of a holiday.

I decided that I had watched a game of bowls at Duntroon Club, why else were they in white? And that the Parliament House had very good toilets and a cafeteria like Coles in Brisbane.

Another boy thought that he had seen a marching girls competition at Duntroon, while still another had a stab at it being the Stations of the Cross. Nobody really understood that claim because the recent holidays were well past Easter.

I don't know if Bradley ever collected his money but he must have done all right because after the next holidays had ended and the Monday bell had rung and we sat down for written expression, Bradley Phie tried to hawk his Canberra ruler again. This time he was met with little demand as most of us had come armed with tourist rulers of our own, even the girl with badges.

One boy who didn't get the ruler in time had a variation on the theme and had instead used a Jacaranda atlas, deciding he had gone on holiday to Africa. His case was made a bit more colourful by referencing local knowledge to flesh out his holiday.

'The Congo is very much like Burpengary on a quiet day. And Cape Town is not quite as big as Sandgate.'

The teacher never said anything, but did make an amount of fuss over our spelling.

It was obvious that a lesson had been learnt. Nobody minded that much if you made up your holidays. And the idea had been planted that for a holiday to be a holiday it had to be away from your home.

It was all right for some. But it came to me on the way home that perhaps the reason my father was worried about the cost of the budgie popes and the reason we didn't really go to Canberra to play bowls at the Duntroon Club was because we didn't have that much money to spare on such things.

The girl with the red hair and badges suddenly looked like she lived life in the fast lane, and I had to admit I couldn't remember the last time I even went to Kallangur.

●

I never really seemed to do that much with my holidays: there were no epic Huckleberry Finn hijinks or *Swallows and*

Amazons adventures, just lower-grade general junior boofhead behaviour.

Not that my holidays were filled with nothing. There was fishing and the beach and the bay. Arsing about in Hayes Inlet in the hire boats before you were caught on the mudflats was a hoot.

And my mother always said the best thing you could do on a holiday was to get yourself a cracking book and have a good read.

But still, it wasn't going away for a holiday.

I had a habit of whingeing a fair bit about there being not much to do when more and more of my friends and schoolmates seemed to be going away to exotic places on holiday.

One friend went all the way to Maryborough.

What did he do?

'Not much, sat round, went for a drive and watched telly,' he said.

'Was it fun?' I asked.

'Yeah, it was all right.' Of course it didn't make any difference that those were the things he did in Redcliffe, too; the fact that he was doing them somewhere else began to loom large in my mind.

When I whinged, it began to be a bit tiresome.

'Why don't you go do something with yourself?' my father would boom.

'All my friends have gone away on holiday,' I moaned.

'They can't all have gone away, not everybody goes away,' said my father.

'Yes they have – all of them.'

'Well, where did they all go?'

'Maryborough,' I blurted. Of course, most of them were at home like me but Maryborough might as well have been Monaco to my way of thinking.

'Listen, the only people who go to Maryborough as a group are those happy hand-clappers from next door.' My father pointed to the Church of Christ, which held its services in a senior citizens' hall every Sunday night, with lots of hand-waving and singing that sounded like second-hand Seekers records.

'You want to get some mates who bat for a brand-name religion, son,' my father finished. 'Bloody Maryborough.'

If I whinged too much my mother would organise an event. A holiday event. This opened up a whole new idea of holiday adventure.

Once, when the pest man had come to spray the house and I was told to get out and enjoy the day, I offered the whiny opinion that, 'There's nothing to do.'

It was a red rag to a bull and my mother quickly organised a spot in the Paddle Pop Lion Holiday Camp at Toombul Shopping Town.

It was quite a piece of manoeuvring because an hour later I was deposited at a cage-like area in the middle of the Toombul shopping mall staring at a man in a Paddle Pop lion suit. The Paddle Pop lion was the symbol of the quite lovely ice-creams that I liked but was also a double-edged sword.

The ice-creams themselves were very good but the sticks were a problem. They were the sorts of things that art teachers from school would tell you to collect for craft classes.

These classes consisted of gluing sticks together into various little structures. The more talented students used matchsticks to construct little boxes – which seemed useless to me – or model houses which were then lacquered to provide a shiny finish. But for the clumsy and less gifted students, or the spuds as we called ourselves, paddle-pop sticks were the preferred craft construction item.

My father regarded what I brought home as a slight improvement on my woodwork and manual training efforts, which invariably fell to pieces when used.

He held an awkward-looking box in his hands and appraised my efforts with, 'Not bad – better than that useless bloody scone-cutter. But you're using those big sticks.'

'What do you mean, Colin?' asked my mother.

'He's got these paddle-pop things, not matchsticks. It's like the difference between a house brick and a Besser block. House bricks you use to make houses, Besser blocks you use for public toilets or dodgy flats. Still,' he said, holding my weird box, 'not bad.'

I couldn't argue and I saw his point. I wasn't that handy with craft.

All that ever happened during these classes was that copious amounts of Tarzan's Grip glue became plastered all over our digits and occasionally a paddle-pop stick was stuck to the back of some unfortunate's uniform.

It was amazing that enough of our brain cells survived to make something of ourselves, considering the amount of glue we accidentally inhaled and digested.

Another teacher, a newly arrived South African mathematics master, used to send students out into the schoolyard to collect 'feefty piddle-pup stucks' as punishment for some classroom crime, and always there was the afterthought, 'And *nooo* stucky ones!'

I had no idea what Mr Craig, pronounced Muster Krrrraig by the man himself, did with his collections of piddle-pup stucks but he watched as we counted them up before him on his desk. If the tally was right, Muster Krrrraig would sweep them into a box that he would carry home after school.

My relationship with Paddle Pops was already under a cloud, and could at times be severely strained, and saddled with this history I was to endure a fun-filled forty-five minutes where the piddle-pup lion, who really was a pretty low-rent Humphrey B. Bear, would flap his arms and pat kids on the head as they coloured in their bits of paper.

Except me. I'd have been a good foot taller than the Paddle Pop lion and a good five years older than the other holiday campers. It was excruciatingly embarrassing but seemed to amuse my mum before she went off to do some shopping. It was made a tad worse as the diminutive Mr Paddle Pop lion paid undue attention to the tall awkward boy.

It was made even worse by the fact that Mr Paddle Pop was intent on 'whispering' to me in a loud yell, 'Good boy, good boy – don't hurt Paddle Pop, don't hurt Paddle Pop. I hug you, don't you hug me – good boy!'

Whatever experience Mr Paddle Pop had previously had must have been memorable for he was on his guard against tall, awkward skinny boys.

'Poor sod must be a bit simple,' I heard someone from the mall say. Whether it was about the flapping Paddle Pop lion or me I didn't know but I assumed it was directed to me and tried to make myself disappear.

I sat hunched in a circle with my barely walking, newfound Paddle Pop chums and coloured in Paddle Pop lion's stupid head with a safari hat atop it.

He patted me vigorously on my head.

'Good boy, good boy. Look, you haven't gone outside the lines at all! Good boy, I'll hug you but you don't hug me. Good boy.'

It wouldn't have been so bad if he hadn't paid so much attention to me.

After the forty-five minutes had finished, me and my other tiny playmates were left waiting in a little pen where our mothers would come and collect us.

I stood holding my colouring-in sheet of the Paddle Pop lion on safari in Africa.

Some mothers thanked me for looking after their children so well, making Paddle Pop do a double-take in our direction.

When my mum came back she told me to watch myself, because people might get the wrong idea.

'Are you supposed to be in there with those toddlers? You might get into trouble.'

When I explained that these were my Paddle Pop playmates my mother stared at me as if someone was playing a joke. She was about to apologise when the Paddle Pop lion came over and hugged me.

'Is he your boy? He's a good, good boy.'

'Get your dirty bloody paws off him, you great rat of a thing,' said my mother. 'You can never tell what sort of people get dressed up in those things. They're as bad as scoutmasters,' she added, to me and anybody else within earshot. What she had against scoutmasters was beyond me but it was invariably followed by 'Bloody Calvinists!'

Paddle Pop lion was suitably stunned as we walked through the mall.

My mother burst out laughing. 'Sorry about that, but you will whinge so much. My god, you were twice the bloody size of them.' She poked me. 'Oh, do stand up straight – and whatever you bloody do,' my mother snarled, 'never ever accept a job that makes you dress up!'

I turned and looked at Paddle Pop lion staring after us with his pith helmet and his paws on his hips. I almost felt sorry for him but as he stared with his great vacant eyes as shoppers swarmed all around him, he seemed a little unnerving.

Years later, I was at Disneyland with my own son, whom I gleefully tortured by having him pose in a series of photographs with lots of people dressed up in Mickey Mouse, Minnie Mouse, Goofy, Baloo, and Donald Duck suits.

His smiles waned as he towered above them all, even Goofy, which I pointed out as I took every photo. When I showed my mother the collection she said simply, 'Bloody scoutmasters!'

•

There followed a series of holiday activities that never quite worked out despite my mother's best efforts. Despite any mother's best efforts, really. All across Australia there were schemes, plans, events – *activities* – that were designed to entertain holidaying children and get them out of their parents' hair for a few hours a day.

Basket weaving, pottery, painting, orienteering, craft design, woodwork and holiday swim camps. Almost any activity that could be thought of to eat up holiday time got a run in the suburbs of Australia.

A day-long body-building and health 'tutorial' held down in an arts hall on a rainy holiday turned out to be run by an elderly man dressed in a white singlet and cricket trousers, with leather shoes, and his wife.

He stank of mints and alcohol and she was deaf as a post and smoked like a chimney.

A dozen or so kids with nowhere else to go during the holiday collected on the bare boards of the hall. As soon as we lined up we knew that we were holiday-less and bereft of any suitable activity. The lowest of the holiday low.

The elderly man spoke in a very deep voice that echoed around the hall. At first I thought it was to frighten us but after a while I realised that it was loud so his wife could hear him.

They were a Mr and Mrs Mellit and were going to guide us in a tutorial of health and fitness exercises.

Mr Mellit had a very broad and flat nose that made a bit of a hiss when he spoke, courtesy of years engaging in his hobby, the gentlemanly art of boxing.

'My face has seen more canvas than Bullen's circus!' said Mr Mellit.

Mrs Mellit looked to him and said, 'Fifteen!'

Mr Mellit turned to her. 'Talking about my nose!'

'Fifteen, fifteen of them,' said Mrs Mellit.

He had greying red hair Brylcreemed into a Mr Whippy quiff and a lower lip that seemed to roll under and then out, like the stomach of a belly dancer, as he thought about what he was going to say.

He was staring at his wife, rolling his lower lip, and she stood staring back at him.

'Fifteen!' she yelled again.

He nodded.

He clapped his hands.

'Well, here we are!'

'Fifteen!'

Some of us knew each other and made a tacit unspoken agreement not to acknowledge this fact. In the group was a strange boy from my school who talked into a stone as if it were a radio and pretended he knew Steve Austin, the Six Million Dollar Man, and Steve's friend and boss, the heavily toupeed Oscar Goldman.

He would walk along the fence at school at lunchtime by himself talking into his hand. He didn't have many friends. He didn't have any, I suppose, and for him to be there with the rest of us on the holidays just hammered home the hopelessness of our situation.

If the boy who talked to a rock was doing the same things as me on holiday, where did that leave me?

I saw that he was whispering. Into his radio rock. 'We are here, Steve, out.'

'You right there, chief?' enquired Mr Mellit.

Mrs Mellit looked at the boy as well, who muttered something about 'contact about to cut' into his rock radio.

'Are you talking to me, young fellow?' asked Mrs Mellit. 'You there?'

The boy's eyes darted to and fro.

He slowly held his rock radio halfway between up and down, so it seemed as though he was giving a clenched-fist 'Hail Caesar' salute.

'Are you saying something? Are you right? Who are you talking to, love?' asked Mrs Mellit.

She walked over to him. 'Is your arm sore? Is it sore? You should have written down if it was sore.'

She turned to her husband. 'I don't think he's got a note.'

'You right there, chief?' repeated Mr Mellit.

The Six Million Dollar Man's friend glanced down at the boards and still held his Hail Caesar salute.

He thrust his rock radio back to his mouth and whispered, 'Out.'

Mrs Mellit was beside herself.

'Are you talking to me, love? What's in your hand? What is it?'

She tried to take the rock but the boy pushed it deep into the pocket of his Stubbies shorts.

'You've got a rock? You're talking to the rock! You shouldn't have a rock.' She looked at her husband. 'You want to watch this one.'

Mr Mellit wheezed through his nose.

The rain fell on the roof and we holiday-less ones stood on the bare boards and enjoyed our holiday activity.

Mr Mellit never took his eyes off the boy with the rock for the rest of what was supposed to be a day we were all to spend together.

It all went slightly off kilter.

Mr Mellit had a bullworker, a few dumbbells and two Indian clubs. He fiddled about with the contraptions, kicked at them with his feet, wheezed through his nose and decided upon the Indian clubs.

He whirled them around like an old plane's spinning propeller, saying in his foghorn voice that, 'All the great athel-leets use these things.' We marched around in circles, did breathing exercises and then followed him in a series of physical manipulations.

We tried our best to copy a few exercises that were shown to us, which seemed to all be variations on the theme of jumping with our legs and swinging our arms with scissor-like movements back and forth.

At one point I went to visit the toilet and when I walked back into the hall it seemed a bit like a James Bond film where a door is opened to a room full of people all doing exercises together and yelling. Perhaps a few judo throws, some staff fighting or heads exploding.

Only this James Bond scene was completely wrong and all over the shop, with limbs going to every direction of the compass and no neat judo throws to be seen. And the only exploding head was Mrs Mellit's, going off about no note and rocks in pockets.

Still, Mr Mellit kept a fair pace and appeared fit. Apparently some of the mothers in the Humpybong Primary tuckshop on midweek soup day said he had been a circus acrobat for years, and had performed at the Ekka in the main arena. Mrs Mellit had been a very good dancer 'in the shows' and 'still gave lessons here and there'.

It was only tuckshop chitchat according to my mum but it made some sort of sense as to why Mr Mellit could contort himself in all sorts of directions. So much so that things began to move internally.

He was doing a pedalling exercise, lying on his back with his legs egg-beating in the air, when the first fart growled out from his bum.

Farting from grown-ups wasn't unknown. My father let rip occasionally, when away from 'the ladies', and added a little Dad coda, as all fathers seem to do – in his case it was either, 'And merry Christmas to you' or 'Cop that'.

But unknown grown-ups who farted were almost unheard of and at first we were stunned. The only sound was the rain and the hiss from Mr Mellit's nose.

The silence was then broken by Mr Mellit saying, 'And here comes the cavalry!' And he farted again.

Some of us laughed, then tried to stop, which made us laugh even harder. I like to think that the Six Million Dollar Man's friend called Steve and Oscar on his rock radio but I wasn't looking, so I couldn't say.

There followed a series of euphemisms for passing wind that would put the *Oxford Dictionary* to shame.

A handstand elicited another emission of noise and was dismissed by Mr Mellit with a nasal hiss and, 'Don't let the mud trumpet bother you.' Other contortions elicited ripsnorters, a thunder pie, ''Scuse the talking pants', and 'There goes a high speed mosquito'.

All the while, Mrs Mellit would be prowling about, talking in a shriek. 'Now what have you done with the rock, love? Watch yourself with that.'

We got to lunchtime and then, for some reason, Mr Mellit looked pained, took a deep breath and seemed suddenly very old.

He nodded to his wife, who walked over to him and put her hand on his shoulder and gently rubbed her palms in small circles. She smiled a little then clapped her hands and decided it was time for a picnic.

She disappeared across the road and came back with dim sims – the big heavy ones with the thick yellow pastry – and chips with sauce and vinegar.

We washed them down with lemonade and sarsaparilla, then we were told to go home early, as Mr Mellit needed a bit of a kip.

And that was the end of our health and fitness tutorial.

Even better was the Arts camp held at the Redcliffe Showgrounds that all artistic and creative children were urged to attend. That basically meant any kid who hadn't gone away for the holidays and whose parents were busy at work or didn't want anybody hanging around the house.

At least the Six Million Dollar Man's friend wasn't one of the artistic and creative kids, which seemed a shame because if anyone was creative it was him. Nevertheless, we all gathered in a suitably creative space at the showgrounds: the area in between the beer shed and the woodchop yard.

We were taught how to paint faces, make masks from breakfast cereal boxes, and circus skills – which meant juggling and walking on stilts, storytelling and the basis of dance and theatre.

Sounds impressive and, well, creative. The stilts looked like they'd been made by my father in a hurry out of bits and pieces of stuff he'd found around the side of the house. They weren't very high but were heavy, with bolts that stuck out into your shins, and for some reason the clumsiest kids were the keenest to use them.

The masks were interesting. We creative and artistic children simply cut out the front or back of cereal boxes, poked holes for our eyes and mouths, threaded through some elastic at the sides and there we had our drama masks.

The people taking the arts camp all had rather ornate masks that were coloured and detailed, and which many years later I recognised as coming from the Madame Tussauds House of Wax in London, whereas all our efforts were more rudimentary.

There was no adornment to the masks, so we ran around screaming with our drama masks of Rice Bubbles, Wheaties, Weet-bix, Froot Loops, Coco Pops and the frightening Shredded Wheat.

'Just like the old Greeks used to use,' said our leader, a balding fat man with pallid eyes who strummed a ukulele. 'These masks are the elemental human emotions – happiness, anger, sorrow.'

He may have had something there because when you are being yelled at by someone in a Kellogg's Raisin Bran mask intimating that, 'I will bash you up, bash you UP!' or listening to a girl crying that she is so lonely in a Coco Pops mask – where you could see one of her eyes through the Coco-lossal monkey's head – it had quite an effect.

It certainly made breakfast more interesting for a while.

The Coco Pops crier was a pretty girl who tried hard and was terribly keen, especially at dance. Another tutor, a tall mournful woman with braided hair and clown's make-up painted on her face, played a flute while the fat balding man strummed his ukulele to an old medieval tune. 'Greenslopes,' he joked. Then we were instructed to 'free dance' on the grass.

The Coco Pops crier, who was wearing tap shoes, attempted an energetic time step that she proudly said she had learnt at the Sharon Alback Dance Centre.

It was delightfully odd and all came together with a performance on the final day that utilised the standing woodchop blocks. Amazingly, a couple of parents attended.

The tutors did most of the storytelling and acting in their Madame Tussauds masks.

The balding fat man began by placing his hand into the small pocket cut into the trunk of a tree-felling pole left over from the woodchops. It was the spot into which the woodchopper would put a plank to continue his way up the trunk.

He told us this pocket was the mouth of a monster and he wailed about having to pay the monster rent for telling stories. The rent was his hand. The only way he could save his hand was if somebody else could pay the rent and the only payment the monster would accept was a story.

'Who here will tell a story? Who will tell a story to satisfy the monster?' he cried.

And then he yelled a bit extra. At first we thought it was acting but then it became clear it wasn't.

'Shit! Oooo, shit, my finger – I got a splinter under my nail!'

He apologised and the performance was suspended while all masks, both breakfast cereal and Madame Tussauds, turned and watched the daubing of Dettol on the wounded fingernail.

Then on with the show, until a fat boy and I were told off for pretend-drinking at the bar, with the watching parents mumbling, 'Oh, poor form!'

In my Rice Bubbles mask I asked, 'How can we pay the rent?'

Here my creative and artistic holiday friend decided to ad-lib and I was told by the fat boy, in a Nabisco Puffed Wheat effort, 'Stuff the rent. We should just get some XXXX. Yeah, let's just sink some pee!'

We were made to apologise to the parents from behind our masks even though the fat boy wasn't sure what he'd done that was wrong.

'You told us we should tell stories from our real lives,' he said to the tutors. 'Well, that's what my dad would have done!'

A loud girl on stilts crashed into somebody juggling tennis balls, scraped her shins and cried so the Dettol was called for again.

The monster was appeased only when the pretty Coco Pops crier, still wearing tap shoes, did a dance to 'The Monster Mash' – an old Sharon Alback Dance Centre favourite.

She bowed before anybody applauded.

The two parents took the cue and stood, continuing a little too long in applauding her, so it was easy to see whose mum and dad had turned up.

The show finished with the tall mournful woman reciting an E. E. Cummings poem, 'Who Knows If the Moon's [a balloon]'.

And that was it. Another holiday activity completed.

We were told we could keep our masks if we wanted, but all of us, I think, even the pretty girl, put them in the bin.

'What will you do now? You going to keep telling stories?' the mournful woman asked us.

Nobody said anything except me. 'I'm going to watch the cricket on the telly.'

And she nodded slowly in her clown make-up.

And I walked home, not realising how much fun I'd had just staying put and not going away for holidays.

•

As I walked home from the showgrounds on that Friday arvo I knew that the last weekend of the school holidays was almost upon me.

If a normal Sunday was tinged with a fatalistic end before school on Monday then it was nothing compared to the sadly desperate feeling that veiled the last weekend of school holidays. The idea that the glory of the holiday break, which seemed to stretch forever, could end, was impossible to believe.

It was a little bit like the end of an empire. Even though cold evidence stares you in the face, somehow denial seems so much sweeter. Perhaps that feeling shrouded the last weekend of the Roman and British empires. It certainly shrouded my Redcliffe Empire as those last two days crept along.

It was frustrating because in my mind there was always so much left undone from the holidays, so much potential unfulfilled. When you're young, days stretch on and the world takes forever to turn. Only later, when we realise that time, that unchanging certainty by which we measure our lives, sweeps on leaving us behind, do we understand how precious our days can be.

Nothing to be too sad about, just something to be aware of, especially on the last weekend of the school holidays.

The World Beyond

There was a point when I realised that the Redcliffe Peninsula wasn't the centre of the universe and that even though it was true that people did come to Redcliffe for holidays it didn't necessarily mean that everyone followed suit.

I think it began in the year that I was taught by a Mr Christensen and I began to amuse myself with an occasional pastime that was the Kosy Korner caravan park run.

The Kosy Korner caravan park was one of the three caravan parks on the peninsula that offered what I thought to be the height in holiday accommodation. I half expected it to feature in a Peter Stuyvesant cigarette advertisement at the old fibro Bay Cinema during a school holiday screening. These were the ads that seemed out of place in a matinee but always got a run, where glamorous people sat around and did glamorous things as they enjoyed a drag on Stuyvie fags in glamorous locations, enjoying 'the international passport to smoking pleasure'.

True, I had never seen anybody from Redcliffe look remotely like these glamorous people but if they were going to turn up anywhere then the Kosy Korner caravan park was as good a place as any for Peter Stuyvesant types, especially considering its unique spelling.

People smoked in those international passport fag ads, and usually drank, too. The way my parents talked about the Kosy Korner, I was pretty sure that drinking and smoking went on there. And perhaps other things from the world of international passports; maybe they played backgammon in the amenities block, in dinner jackets and gowns with plunging necklines decorated with strings of pearls.

Why stop at ciggy ads? Maybe they were like the people who would occasionally appear in the *Sunday Mail* photo section of the rich and glamorous. Maybe they were men who, like Omar Sharif and Roger Moore, raised eyebrows and brandy glasses and said smart things. And if not those two, then perhaps like Bernard King, or Ken Lord or Don Seccombe, the newsreader from Channel Nine, and Annette Allison, the weather girl. Perhaps they would bring a bit of Mount Coot-tha Brisbane magic to the amenities block.

The fact that Omar and Roger and the local gang wouldn't be found in the dear old Kosy Korner caravan park soon became pretty obvious. In fact, that the Kosy wasn't ever going to be the sort of place where you enjoyed the international passport to anything much dawned on me suddenly in the most striking of circumstances.

It was a school holiday afternoon and I was going down to the book exchange with some war comics when I bumped into a boy called Gary Hodges, who looked slightly alarmed. I didn't really say anything to him because I knew he was half tough and used to spit a lot. But he stared at me, wide eyed, and said, 'Dare you to walk through the caravan park.'

I stared back at him.

He spat and yelled, 'Dare you!'

I was bigger than him though he was older.

He pointed to the rather homemade-looking sign over the entrance, a black silhouetted caravan on a blue background and the bold black lettering of 'Kosy Korner caravan park'.

Underneath hung a sign written by a less professional hand, 'Permanents welcome.'

Gary's dare didn't seem to amount to much and I thought it was as good a time as any to match myself against a half tough in the young rooster stakes.

I nodded to him and walked into the world of Kosy Korner.

Within about fifteen metres of entering that world I was pretty sure I wouldn't find any Peter Stuyvesant people.

Somebody from a dark caravan hawked spit like a cracking

whip and then there was a slap twice as loud. 'Not inside, you pig.'

Somebody else swore.

I suddenly had second thoughts about the dare and turned back. Gary Hodges was leering at me.

So I kept going. A man covered in tatts came out of an annex and flung the canvas flap like an Arab sheik from *Lawrence of Arabia*.

He had a scar across his forehead and dark eyes. He wore Stubbies and nothing else. Except his tattoos and an earring in his left ear. He belched loudly and stared at me.

I nearly wet myself.

Then he nodded. Belched again and said, 'How ya going?'

I stared.

He scratched himself and spoke again. 'Give you the change if you go down to the Ambass for a six-pack and a bottle of port.'

He meant the two-storey fibro Ambassador Hotel on the beachfront, the rear entrance of which backed onto Sutton Street, on the other side of Kosy Korner.

He looked at me. I stared.

I was about to try to say something when I dropped a comic from my hand.

It was a Commando comic, with a snarling man with a grenade and a gun. 'This man is dangerous.'

It seemed a little too apt.

I bent down and picked up my comic.

Then I heard a growl. It stopped. I slowly rose. The growl started again. I stopped. The growl stopped. I kept on rising, the growling continued.

I was half bent over, looking at the tattooed man in the Stubbies who was scratching himself. Where was the growling coming from and why did it stop when I stopped? The Stubbies man went to speak.

He held up his arm, opened his mouth and a sneeze exploded from his nose and mouth.

I jumped up. The growling began again.

A woman screamed.

'MINTY! Minty!'

I turned in fright and saw a dog with bared teeth standing on the step of a silver caravan. A woman grasped at him. She was wearing a nightie and slippers and puffing on a cigarette.

I ran.

And Minty ran after me. And the woman in her nightie puffing on a fag ran after Minty.

I ran like a madman around the caravan park, past caravans and tents and dusty little cabins.

The dog leapt at me.

The woman was screaming. 'Minty! Minty, Minty! Stop running! Stop it!'

It was like some awful ride at the show. Forget the ghost house ride, try the Kosy Korner Run.

The dog nipped me once and I screamed.

The woman dropped her smoke and stopped to pick it up,

howling, 'You bag of shit!' I wondered if the fag was a Peter Stuyvesant. Something told me it probably wasn't.

I ran past the man in the tatts and Stubbies, waving almost unimaginably a twenty-dollar note at me as if it were the chequered flag in some race.

The woman screamed, 'Minty!' And then after me, 'You dickhead, stop running!'

I ran though the entrance, past Gary Hodges, who spat at me and called me a dickhead as well.

Then he got his, as Minty snarled at him. He tried to aim a kick in the dog's direction but the nightie woman picked up Minty and had a go at Gary Hodges.

There was a crack, a 'Screw ya' and a cry, and then Gary Hodges ran off past me and across the road in tears.

I felt that somehow my rooster feathers were half earned even though I'd run away and screamed because at least I hadn't cried at Kosy Korner.

Later when I got home I asked my father what sort of people lived at the Kosy Korner and if all the people who stayed in caravan parks were the same.

'What were you doing in the Kosy Korner?' he snapped.

I stared at him.

He sounded like the sheriff in some Western asking what was I doing in the saloon.

'A boy dared me,' I said.

'What did you do?'

'Tried to walk through. Minty chased me.'

My father shook his head. 'Who the bloody hell is Minty?'

'Minty bit me.'

'Have you heard what your bloody son's up to?'

My mother was informed of my dare.

'You don't want to be walking through Kosy Korner,' she said. 'And don't you go thinking you are any better than anybody that lives there. But you don't want to walk through there for no reason.'

'Aren't they on holiday?'

'Yeah, from life.'

My father shook his head. 'Holiday? Son, these days the Kosy Korner is where you go when you can't live in Kippa-Ring. The place is full of permanents.'

'Colin!' said my mother.

'You don't do well at school and that's where you'll end up – in the Kosy Korner!'

'What's a permanent?' I asked.

'Permanent bloody resident!' said my father.

Both my parents laughed. 'Listen, you,' said my father, 'that place is just a place where people live. Okay?'

I nodded and the idea of the Kosy Korner being a holiday spot waned considerably.

Permanents.

Occasionally though, I would walk through the Kosy Korner to test my courage. Minty growled from the old silver caravan and sometimes barked but never chased me. His owner, who was always in that nightie and smoked what turned out to be Escort cigarettes, would tell Minty to 'Shush up, you mongrel.'

And once I went and got a six-pack and a bottle of port from the Ambass for the man in tatts and Stubbies shorts.

He turned out to be named Karl.

'Fanks,' he said and disappeared back inside the annex.

I kept the change.

The last time I walked through I half waited for him to swing open the flap of his annex, like Lawrence of Arabia.

It didn't happen.

Minty growled and I heard a voice. It was the nightie lady, Escort in her mouth. 'Your mate has shot through. Must have known the coppers were after him.'

Then she turned back into the caravan and yelled at Minty.

Later, when I was older and not as funny as I thought I was, as a joke I'd run through the Kosy Korner caravan park and yell, 'Police! Police!' and see how many people would try to scarper from the old vans.

Many years later during a book event in Sydney I mentioned that I'd grown up in Redcliffe.

A man approached me, holding a book of mine to sign.

'You from Redcliffe?' he said slowly.

'Yes,' I confirmed.

'Yeah? You ever heard of the caravan park on Anzac Avenue in Redcliffe?'

I laughed. 'The old Kosy Korner!'

He stared at me. 'I went there with my mum on a holiday.'

I stared at him.

'For a night.'

I tried not to laugh.

'It was a nightmare,' the man said. 'Our car had broken down and we had to stay the night. It was like something out of a horror film.'

'Yeah?' I said.

'Still,' said the man, 'it was sort of good. My mum apologised to me for years after. And she never liked you on the telly either.' He laughed.

I asked if anybody at the caravan park had had a dog that barked called Minty.

He shook his head. 'But the police were there, running around screaming things out.'

'Like what?'

'Just, "Police! Police!" They gave Mum a fright but then she said they were just nongs of kids hooning around.' He laughed again.

I should have told him his mother was dead right.

•

Mr Christensen thought I was a nong of a kid too.

He wasn't a bad teacher and had the reasonable expectation that students should try to learn things. He didn't think much of me. On one of my school reports, Mr and Mrs McInnes were informed that their youngest son was 'quite bright but has an inability to sit still and a tendency to speak drivel and use slang in written expression'.

He was also the teacher who blurred the lines between school and holiday in more ways than I thought possible, and confirmed that there was life away from the peninsula.

During a history lesson, for example, he put the European colonisation of Australia into context for us.

The whole penal settlement was like a holiday camp.

'Well, some English folk decided to come for a holiday and they stayed here in Redcliffe but decided they liked Brisbane a bit better and went off over there,' and he waved his hand. 'So there we are, a unique way of looking at penal settlement and colonisation; as a holiday tour.'

I think he was being a bit dry but you never knew with Mr Christensen.

He was a neat man, who had horn-rimmed glasses and in summer wore short-sleeved white shirts, ties and pressed shorts and long socks. In winter, it was grey trousers and a cardigan.

He was also quite strict and became something of a legend when he smacked a girl in calipers for being naughty. I can't remember what the offence was but it must not have been that bad because she was a pretty well-behaved girl. True, she had 'married' a boy called Brian Christopher in a lunchtime ceremony in an earlier grade, which I found odd. They were only playing a game but went into great detail, enlisting a best man, bridesmaids, flowers and even a veil.

I don't know how long the 'marriage' lasted, because it wasn't much time before Brian was plying his trade as one of the primary school's all-time great underarm farters.

In fact, after the ceremony, before they walked away, he farted quickly under both arms, a beautiful retort to celebrate the whole event.

His bride's name was Cherry Barber and I don't know whether she was that upset when Mr Christensen struck her because it was only a gentle tap that – I think – was supposed to mean that she wasn't going to be treated any differently to the rest of us.

I knew it was gentle because I was aware of Mr Christensen's form. He occasionally let me have a pretty decent stroke across the back, which proved his credentials as the head of tennis at Humpybong.

Once, during his pre-holiday ritual of reading to us, he gave me a fair old forehand drive across my back.

He liked reading to us, which I thought pleasant. Other teachers would make us read books standing in front of the class, which was as boring as bat shit, really; kids would get nervous and mumble words they couldn't pronounce and some would stare at the book, hardly comprehending what it was they were supposed to be reading.

But it seemed Mr Christensen could not let go of the performing bug and away he'd go.

He liked to read Australian stuff to us. He introduced me to Colin Thiele's *February Dragon*. It was exciting and moving and startling to kids our age – even one like me with an inability to sit still. He did some accents as he read, which I thought all sounded the same, but it was still wonderful because a grown-up was having a go.

That's why I didn't take it personally when he belted me during a Banjo Paterson poem.

He'd read two bush ballads, which when you're that age are pretty good, especially the lyrics to 'Waltzing Matilda'. I had always been partial to the tale of the swagman and the jumbuck, and when Mr Christensen said that swagmen used to live rough, I thought that meant that if the swaggie was around today he'd head to the Kosy Korner caravan park.

Maybe he was even covered in tatts or had a little yappy dog.

I liked the swaggie so much that one holiday when I was a bit smaller, I joined the Jolly Swagman Club – the brainchild of somebody from Ampol.

Ampol was the only petrol station conglomerate that was Australian. Golden Fleece, my old man always said, was really owned by Caltex. Caltex, Mobil and Esso were all American, BP was British, Shell was Dutch and the mysterious Total was French.

Total was mysterious because the only servo it seemed to have in Australia was in Burpengary. And the only person to admit going there was my aunt. She joked that she'd drive from Deception Bay and make her old VW more sophisticated with a bit of French oil.

French sophistication in Burpengary. Mysterious.

My father said he would go to Ampol if Ken MacCohan and his Robin Hood gang were too busy.

We must have gone there sometime and I ended up joining Aussie Ampol's marketing exercise – the Jolly Swagman Club. As a member, I received a plastic bag with a freckly cork-hatted swagman on the outside. Inside was a jigsaw, a plastic boomerang and an orange plastic record with 'Waltzing Matilda' and a rather loud would-be national howler called 'God Bless Australia' that rolled along to the tune of 'Waltzing Matilda'.

The jigsaw didn't last long, I threw the boomerang at one of my sisters and it ended up in the bin, but that plastic record hung around for years.

The orange record version of 'Waltzing Matilda' wasn't as memorable as the renditions of Banjo's poems that were sonorously and almost hypnotically intoned from radiograms during holiday time by Australian actor Leonard Teale, who also appeared in TV's *Homicide*.

'That *Homicide* bugger would sound the same underwater,' was my father's verdict.

In grade six at Humptybong, Mr Christensen was doing a fair job of outdoing Watery Homicide Leonard with his reading of 'The Man from Snowy River'.

Until the pause. Near the end when the man from Snowy River and his pony are bulleting down the slopes, there's a pause; a dramatic pause. Which I unfortunately filled. With a cracking fart.

A real howler that at another time I would've been proud to claim – but this one, like many a great work of art, was totally unintentional. It didn't make it any better that the preceding line was, 'At the bottom of that terrible descent'.

To say I received a healthy reception at the office from Mr Stevens and the cane is an understatement.

•

Mr Christensen, as a special treat after the exams for that year were finished, decided it might be fun to talk about holidays.

Shockingly, he showed us slides of his holidays.

The slide show, which seemed to last as long as winter and was just as bleak, sank an afternoon.

I watched as another person's holiday flashed before my eyes. In almost every slide his family was arranged in front of a series of landmarks somewhere. I think Mr Christensen showed us his holiday slides because he thought it would be nice for us to see the world outside of Redcliffe.

There was no familiar landmark to be seen, but we guessed it must have been somewhere in Australia. It was all rather spooky. With a Holden station wagon in every image, Mr Christensen and his wife and children stood in front of a rock, a dam, a bridge, a river, a shopping centre, a desert, a drive-in, a cow and a boat before there was an almost hypnotic shot of all of them, including Mr Christensen with his horn-rimmed glasses shimmering in the light, with their eyes closed in front of nothing but a blue horizon.

It was an eerie, almost ghostly image that haunted my dreams. A family holiday. How far had they driven in that Holden station wagon? How many odd stops were made for a photo opportunity? Just sitting there watching the never-ending series of slides made you feel as if you'd been with them. Almost to the extent of wanting to ask, 'Are we there yet?' but in a terrified way because nobody knew where we were going.

'I need to go to the toilet,' a kid whispered but Mr Christensen said levelly, 'You can go after we get to bauxite terminal. We stopped for you a moment ago.'

He was talking about the slide of the bauxite terminal, of course, but it was as if he was reliving the whole holiday with us.

Occasionally he would stop and stare at a slide, saying nothing before turning the carousel. Once, when they were at some beach, the family again lined up like the Romanovs before the revolutionary Russian guards, Mr Christensen stared at the image, made a humming sound and then pressed the next slide.

It was of the same beach with just his wife in a white cotton dress holding her glasses in her hand. She was half turning back to the camera, as if her name had been called, looking half surprised but happy. She was smiling.

I wondered who had said what to her and as Mr Christensen gazed at it he smiled to himself.

The kid asked again if she could go to the toilet. 'Pleeeease, sir.'

Mr Christensen said nothing. He was still smiling. Then he stopped and switched off the slides.

'Yes,' he said, 'be quick about it.'

And as the girl tumbled out of the classroom, knocking tables and chairs out of her way, and thumping down the verandah, Mr Christensen gave a lasting bit of wisdom about holidays before that school year ended.

'Holidays are funny things. Sometimes it's enough to know that you've had them, that you don't have to have a photo or a badge or even a story to tell. It's enough to know you've lived them.'

He stared at us almost as if he were looking at his holiday slides and then said goodbye.

•

Viewing Mr Christensen's slides was a shocking experience because I had never considered that teachers had holidays. Or even families or lives outside what they did from nine till three. I felt uneasy knowing that a teacher had another real life outside the classroom. It made him seem more human.

Even though I never saw Mr Christensen in real life outside school, it always slightly unnerved me thereafter to see other teachers on holidays. It may have humanised them, but it was never quite right.

When I was a high school student I was once accosted on my way home by a Maths teacher who saw fit to try to threaten me with school discipline during the middle of the holidays.

I had a face full of acne and looked like a toilet brush. It was all because I had been sent to the barber's to get a haircut on the orders of a sports master on the last day of the previous term. This man deemed my hair too long and I was given a note and also a verbal send-off as to what to do.

The sports master loved to yell and I thought he was going

to break his throat screaming at me next term when he saw what had happened.

I went to the barber in good faith but was somehow talked into having a perm by a lovely girl who was a trainee hairdresser there.

So I walked out from the barber with this ridiculous hairstyle and ran into a Maths teacher in holiday gear. He had bushwhacked me by coming from the Piccadilly Cafe in a pair of tight aqua shorts, which were way too short, and a wife-beater singlet. In his hand was a freshly purchased crumbed sausage. In his other hand was a copy of a blokey magazine called *Pix People* with a girl in a bikini on the cover.

Pix People could be best described as a poor man's *Playboy* magazine and the sight of it in this teacher's hands was amusing enough for me to snap out of my daze and offer a thought.

'Bit of dunny reading on your holiday, sir?'

He seethed and clenched his crumbed sausage.

These crumbed sausages were deep-fried bits of manufactured meat filled with some yellow goo which was supposedly a dairy product.

The Maths teacher was a friend and ally of the sports master and he pointed an accusatory crumbed sausage at me with such violence that the end of it broke off and he got even more annoyed as gooey yellow pus dripped onto his thonged feet.

'McInnes – you clown. After a job at Bullen's with that hair? Don't bring it to school.'

Thereafter at school the Maths teacher and sports master always referred to me as 'Bullen's', as in Bullen's circus because I was a clown.

I also saw the yelling sports master during the same holidays with his head in his hands at the TAB and then delivering free newspapers from a Mini Moke.

Before I went back to school I had my hair shaved and, even though they yelled at me, they weren't so scary. I knew what they had done in their holidays and it wasn't very much.

But back in grade six when Mr Christensen had finished showing us his holidays slides, and we counted down the last minutes before the arvo bell rang, the grey speakers in the corner of the classroom crackled with an announcement from our grumpy headmaster Mr Stevens.

'Soon you'll be going up a grade and be a year older. Soon school will seem a bit different, soon there will be school trips for you to enjoy. The strange thing is these trips are like holidays with learning. You'll think they'll be fun but you just wait and see where your children will go for their trips compared to you.'

It wasn't until years later when my son went on a school trip one Easter that I understood what my grumpy cane-wielding headmaster had meant. And just how true were the words of my old slide-show-loving teacher.

•

I went on a school trip when I was a student. Actually I went on a few. So did my son. So will my daughter, in fact.

We're all equal on the generational ledger.

Sort of.

My daughter is off on two educational holidays, one to Italy and one to England.

My son went to Nepal to help build a schoolroom in the mountains there. And to trek through the country. To see a culture I couldn't have even imagined when I was a kid. An 'educational holiday' flying through a storm over the mountains in an aircraft run by Yeti Air singing, 'I'll Make a Man out of You' from the film *Mulan* as the plane weaved, dipped and dropped.

He and his schoolmates, a teacher told me, taught a little boy how to kick a Sherrin football 18,000 feet above sea level. The little boy in turn taught my son and his schoolmates not to feed the monkeys. And not to be frightened of the funerals by the rivers.

I suddenly remember Mr Christensen. His slides were a hint that there were whole other worlds out there beyond Hayes Inlet and the long and bumpy bridge. My son's school takes him and his classmates to those other worlds.

It's not like I missed out on anything really and I bet my son never saw anything like Mr Christensen's slides.

And anyway, I did travel a bit. How far?

Me? For my school trip, I went to an island in the mouth of the Brisbane River. It may have been Peel Island or it might have been one that was swallowed by the airport.

We went with a teacher who was an entertaining fantasist – the sort of fellow who boasted he was descended from James

Cook and had helped Edmund Hillary as well as Tenzing Norgay and anybody else who might have been hanging round at the breakfast table up Mount Everest (even though he'd climbed it twice that morning before either of them had got out of their PJs).

Every school has one.

We walked around the island in about ten minutes. I bought a 1980 hamburger at 2014 prices off a bored guy with bad glasses and a dirty baseball cap.

Our teacher pulled at his carefully trimmed beard – he looked a little like an emaciated version of the ghost from the old TV show *The Ghost and Mrs Muir*, only he didn't have the nice rollneck jumpers, just a funny mustard cardigan that teachers in the late seventies seemed to prefer – and spread his legs out wider as he ordered a discounted egg and lettuce sandwich and said, 'Yes, I was a paratrooper, you know.' The man in the baseball hat couldn't have cared less.

Then we went home.

The trip to the Snowy Mountains in Year 11 was better. Two weeks on a bus wearing jumpers and parkas that would make an Eskimo dehydrate. We saw road kill, turbines, a bloke who made clogs, a bit of snow and more road kill.

When you're on a bus for that long, you slowly devolve into some barely recognisable form of human being. A busload of teenage Neanderthals.

The other highlight was a night when some of us got a few bottles of plonk from a supermarket in Canberra and had a bit of a party.

We all got tiddly, which we thought was pretty cool but was topped when a physical education teacher called Mrs Bust came in pissed as a fart and told us to go to bed and then locked herself in a cupboard and I think went to sleep. She let herself out about half an hour later and never said a word about any of it.

Anyway, this trip discrepancy between my children and me made me think of other great educational holiday trips I went on. An epic trek to Nambour to stand and stare wistfully up at the fibreglass udders of the Big Cow. Then Charlton Boy – a favourite galloper of my family's – was trotted out and drank a can of XXXX beer. Then on to the Big Pineapple and the life-changing trip to the Golden Circle cannery, where a guide ushered us into an area with the words, 'This is where all the excitement is!'

Rows of earnest people with long knives were butchering pineapples.

At least we were given a free glass of juice.

During a Newstead House tour we paraded carefully through Queensland's colonial past, which was topped off with a convict's finger floating in formaldehyde inside what looked like a Masterfood's cayenne pepper jar.

I hear my son's stories of seeing life in Nepal. Funeral pyres in public, of hope and poverty and beauty – stories of a different life. His life, his holidays.

That same year he walked the grounds of Gettysburg, the halls of Washington and the Smithsonian.

I got a call from the father of the family he was staying with in Boston. My son had lost a camera and they would do their best to find it and pass it on.

The man's accent was broad, almost like he was doing a John F. Kennedy impersonation. 'Hey now, your boy, uh, your boy is a good kid. You should be proud of him. He is a good boy.'

'Pardon?' I said. I had heard the man, who happened to be a police chief, apparently, so I had no reason to believe he would be telling an untruth, but I was surprised because quite frankly there have been times in my life where I could have strangled my children.

'How do you mean?' I asked.

'Well, uh, we watched your football team the other morning in a lay-off. What do you guys call it? A final? The Bulldogs.'

I almost groaned. 'Oh, the footy.'

'Yeah, they lost.'

'Yeah, they'll do that to you, the Bulldogs.'

'Yeah?'

'Yeah.'

'Your boy cried.'

'Yeah, they'll do that to you, the Bulldogs.'

He laughed.

'Well, I asked your boy if he was okay and he —' The man laughed. He went on, 'Your boy said that tears you cry over sport aren't that real so you don't have to pay that much attention to them.'

'Right,' I said.

'That's a pretty good thing for a kid to say, you know.'

'I suppose so.'

'Anyway, we got to talking, your boy and me, and uh, I asked what had he seen since he's been over here, and he said, "Washington was good." Uh, so I asked him what he thought of the Lincoln Memorial and he said it was big. So I said, "Do you have anything like that in Australia?"'

I didn't say anything and the chief of police went on.

'And your boy said, no, nothing that big. But he said that America has to have a monument that big to remind us of how great and good we can be, and you know, I thought that was a good thing to say. So I asked your boy, "You don't need anything like that in Australia?" And he says, "No, I don't think so – we've got each other." I go, "Each other?" And he says, "Yeah, each other – our family, our friends, each other."'

'He said that?' I must have sounded incredulous, because he laughed.

'Yeah, he did. Quite a thing to say. You should be proud of him.'

'Well, okay.' I didn't really know what to say. 'Thanks.'

'Hey, you're welcome,' he said.

The camera never made it home but my son did.

There is nothing like going to the airport to pick up a person returning home. You want to see them so much, to hug them, and invariably all they want to do is sleep.

And there is nothing like waiting to pick up your son from an overseas trip when another parent, who looks nervous and a little concerned, comes up to you and asks, 'Is your son going to be suspended too?'

I thought it was a joke and then I could see the poor man was serious.

Then I saw a teacher coming towards us. The nervous parent went to open his mouth and the teacher smiled. 'Whatever you may have heard, don't worry. It's all good, nobody's in strife.'

The nervous parent looked relieved, I looked bewildered.

The teacher smiled. 'William, let me tell you this much: in twenty years' time when reunions start, this trip is something half the boys at school will claim they went on.'

I stared and then laughed.

He nodded. 'Yeah, that good.' And he laughed as well.

Then two great arms surrounded me and it was my son hugging me. Smiling his big smile.

No, the camera didn't make it home, and there were no photos to share, no slide show to see, as it were.

I asked my son how it all went, expecting some explanation of an educational holiday that already seemed to be being etched in legend.

'It was all right.' He shrugged.

I was going to ask for more information when I remembered Mr Christensen. 'It's enough to know you've lived them.'

Each generation learns and builds on the one before. That is how we grow. And it's good. We all earn stories and some we share when the time is right – that's why those stories are the ones worth waiting for and listening to. But I know one thing: I bet my kids won't see a floating convict's finger or a Stradbroke Cup winner drink a can of XXXX.

Proper Holidays

Funbags was the first person of my social circle to earn enough money from her own hard work and endeavour to put it towards a proper holiday.

A proper holiday was one that was purchased with the help and guidance of a travel agent.

I heard the news I think from Kevin Rammer. 'I saw her. I saw Funbags walking out of Jetset travel with the bag and magazine and everything.'

'Where's she heading?'

'Club Med. Club Med in Vanuatu,' he gasped.

'Where?' I said.

'Club Med, she had the bag and everything,' said Kevin almost incredulously. 'She had the Jetset bag and everything.'

Funbags was a tall girl with an awkward gait.

'I knew she'd do something like this,' Kevin continued.

'What?'

'Go to a place like Club Med. It's for young singles, you know.' And he nodded his head up and down and repeated, 'A young singles' place.'

I told Kevin I had never heard him say that Funbags would go to a young singles' place.

'Yeah, I did, I said she'd pose for *Penthouse*.'

I looked at him. He nodded.

'What does posing for *Penthouse* and Club Med have in common?'

'It's the same thing,' he almost cried. 'It's where young singles go and do stuff.'

I looked at him. He was a round red ball of humanity. God knows what he thought the connection between Club Med and *Penthouse* magazine was or why on earth a girl like Funbags would pose in such a publication.

Still, Funbags had gone to Jetset and bought a proper holiday.

Travel agents.

People who knew holidays, who, with a pen in hand and a nameplate on their desk, had the world of travel knowledge at the end of the phone line. People who could show you the way to a proper holiday.

Travel agents used to be the sort of businesses that would be a given in suburbs across Australia. The places that would be a go-to for suburban festivities such as school fetes, fundraisers and charity events to hit up for donations and support.

They were like chemists, butchers or dentists – an almost automatic part of the local suburban landscape. They were usually family-run small businesses and even though the shops were filled with posters of people who were invariably happy being on holiday (more glamorous even than the Peter Stuyvesant folk) the travel agents sitting below would glower at their desks all day long, waiting for the phone to ring.

I know this because when I was at uni, I was friendly with a girl who would go into travel agents and collect the catalogues and never go on any actual holidays.

'Travel agents don't really know what it is they're talking about anyway,' she said as she flipped through a Pacific Islands brochure. 'They just sell people what they're told to sell.'

She should have known as her father, Trevor Tait, ran a travel agency.

He was an anxious man with false teeth and a habit of repeating things. The travel agency he ran was in a corner of a shopping centre. It was airless and quite dark in that corner and, as a consequence, the shop was filled with harsh fluorescent lights that accentuated the pallor of those who worked there against the bright and happy posters that were dotted around the shop.

Trevor's wife also worked at the travel agency, as well as his sister-in-law, whom he detested.

The first time I met him he was sitting beneath a cruise

line poster of a couple kissing alone on a deck bathed in a beautiful sunset.

'Yes, roger that, roger that,' he spoke into the phone as the girl I was friendly with flipped through some catalogues.

Trevor Tait was writing down some notes and staring at a large woman who was trying to catch a fly with her hands. She clapped them together like cymbals at the end of some grand piece of music.

'Yes Fiji, Fiji . . . Fiji it is. They have a marvellous police band in the capital.' Mr Tait never took his eyes off the clapping woman.

She clapped louder and he spoke louder.

'Well, happy to help, to help.'

He finished with a laugh and banged the phone down on the cradle. He looked at me and his daughter and yelled.

'Business call, business call, and somebody's clapping like a halfwit, a halfwit, in my ear, in my ear.'

He stared and there was silence until the woman clapped again.

Not at a fly but very loudly in the direction of Mr Tait and then she sat smiling at him, and he sat staring at us and grinding his jaw.

I noticed that his nameplate was bigger than the ones on the other desks.

The clapping woman sat behind a nameplate, 'Denise', and across from her was a very fit-looking woman who sat behind a similar-sized plaque which said her name was 'Lenore'.

She spoke to Mr Tait.

'Trevor, don't sit there and grind your teeth.'

'I am not, not, grinding my teeth.'

'Oh, Trevor, I can see you doing it. I can see your ears wriggling.'

I looked down at Mr Tait, who stared up at me and his youngest daughter. His ears were wriggling.

'It's very bad for your plates, Trevor, you don't want to crack a set again.'

'It must hurt his gums. Why does he do it?' said Denise and she clapped again.

'A business call, business call!' cried Mr Tait.

He had a name badge on his shirt as well, and it was also bigger than those that the other people wore in the office.

'You must bring back, bring back, those catalogues, love,' he told his daughter. 'They don't grow on trees and they are of this business. They are business literature.'

He looked at his daughter but spoke about me. 'Who's your friend? Your friend?'

His daughter introduced me as she picked up a few more catalogues.

Lenore Tait, her mother, stood and walked over, smiling. 'Well, hello there.' She introduced Aunty Denise, who smiled and clapped at a fly.

The phone rang and Trevor Tait picked it up and barked into it. 'Trevor Tait speaking of Trevor Tait Travel.' He spoke very quickly and clearly.

'You don't need to yell, Trevor, they can hear you, you know. That's what the telephone is for.'

'Well, we certainly, certainly, can help with your holiday enquiry. Certainly, after all, my business is your holidays. Your holidays!' Mr Tait spoke even louder and faster.

Lenore Tait shook her head, let out a little sigh and turned to us, smiling. 'Well, we hope we'll be seeing a bit more of you, William.' And then she added to her daughter, 'Make sure you bring some of those things back, darling,' She pointed to the catalogues. 'You know how he carries on.'

As we walked out I heard another clap. It was the first time that I had been inside a travel agent's office and, as it turned out, it wasn't my last because I did see a bit more of the Taits.

They were all lovely and, like any family, had ways of doing things that probably seemed peculiar to others but that added to their charm.

My friend had two older sisters: Jackie, who was married to a dentist in Townsville, and Donna, who was a year older and very, very pretty. She worked in the travel agency as a receptionist (she had a name tag and a plaque on the front desk – again, it was in lettering much smaller than her father's) between bouts of employment as a model and an entrant in beauty quests.

Occasionally my friend and I would go back to the Tait home during business hours to enjoy ourselves. My friend was quite sporty and an enthusiastic hockey player, much like her mother. But this meant that she was the opposite of her sister Donna who, while a keen attendee of a local gym and with a fair collection of leotards, leg warmers and headbands inspired by Olivia Newton-John and the 'Physical' film clip, was interested in wellbeing and fitness for more aesthetic ends.

The sisters shared a bedroom that was divided down the middle by an invisible demarcation line, which displayed the two girls' personalities and interests.

My friend's side was fairly untidy and littered with shin pads, the odd mouthguard, bits of strapping, books about birds, shoes of a sporting and recreational nature, and a ragged old teddy bear with an eye missing.

Donna's half was clean and ordered. It was nearly all pastel in colour and any shoes that couldn't fit into her inbuilt cupboard were neatly arranged at the bottom of her bed. Upon the bed was an old favourite teddy bear, which was the twin of my friend's battered old teddy, though Donna's was in almost pristine condition and was adorned with a pink ribbon. On the wall alongside her bed were satin sashes of different colours.

These were a series of beauty pageant sashes. Gold, red, green and white. Miss Rugby League, Miss Sun Girl, Miss Personality, Miss this and that, even a Miss Queensland Hardware entrant sash.

My friend had a few small ribbons from hockey and a swag of trophies, some on the floor and some on the shelf.

But it was these sashes that were fascinating.

'She doesn't like people touching them, you know. She goes off her head if she thinks they've been moved.'

So she moved one slightly.

'That's enough to set her off.'

'How many does she have?'

She smiled and slid open the inbuilt cupboard. 'Heaps. She hardly ever wins, but she keeps on trying. And why not? She's pretty.'

I nodded.

My friend picked out a purple Miss Cattleland sash and put it over my shoulders and kissed me. 'I think you look rather nice in that one.' And she laughed.

Thereafter began a rather odd little game of us both wearing her sister's sashes as we exercised together.

We made sure never to use the ones that Donna actually displayed, although occasionally my friend would drape one of these over me if I had 'done well'.

My friend looked at me. She smiled. 'Donna is okay, you know.'

I said I knew that.

'She wants to be a *Sale of the Century* model.'

'What – the ones that show stuff off?'

My friend nodded.

Sale of the Century models showed off the gifts that would tempt the contestants on the popular television quiz show. They would wear a bikini to point to electric eggbeaters or clinging evening dresses to waft hands across barbecues, television sets and, on special occasions, cars. On these, they might even lounge.

My friend wafted her hand over her sister's bed and teddy bear. We both laughed.

Everyone, it seems, has dreams and Donna's didn't seem any more dim than anybody else's. Over the time I knew the Taits, Donna would be in a constant state of rehearsal to prepare for a possible career as a prize temptress on *Sale of the Century.*

She would practise leaning against cars in the drive or typewriters at the office. Sometimes she would display with a flourish of her hands a wooden salad bowl that she had placed on the table at a barbecue, smiling a nice bland model's smile.

'Oh, that's lovely, Donna,' said Mrs Tait, who was almost always dressed in a hockey skirt and blouse. She was mad about the game and had a series of junior and senior teams with which she was connected in some hockey capacity. Most of the time she would be using the travel office to organise newsletters, team lists and social hockey news.

Her sister Denise was a slightly odd woman who seemed to be pleasant enough but was a complete mystery to me and was described by Trevor Tait as being 'Undeniably, undeniably, simple in the head. No rhyme or reason but there we have it, simple in the head. In the head.'

She seemed to clap for no apparent reason and it was one of the many things that drove Trevor Tait up the wall. 'And she's with us, with us, in a room next to my shed and she wanders into all the rooms without knocking, without knocking. I can't fathom it at all. At all.'

He could see some sense in his wife and her sister being 'mad about the bloody hockey thing, but that bloody Denise and her clapping is just too bloody odd. Bloody odd.'

Trevor Tait – patriarch of the Tait brigade, as he liked to refer to his family – was a fascinating man.

He was a strange fellow in an ultimately normal sort of way. He'd served in the army and had never let go of a certain way of speaking. He had an urgency to his behaviour that bordered on frantic but at the same time he did things in such a deliberate manner that he was almost impossible not to watch, even when it was painful.

As well as repeating things incessantly, he loved to use the phonetic radio alphabet, a hangover from his army days, perhaps, that he dropped into casual and business communication.

I bumped into him once at a rugby match where he was sponsoring a prize.

'William, William, William. Good to see you. William, Whiskey India Lima Lima India Alpha Mike, how are you?'

Whether it was a habit or just a party trick I could never really tell.

Sometimes he would swear according to the radio alphabet when he didn't want to appear too blue in front of particular company.

'Well now, well now, it's plain to see that this particular fellow is a Foxtrot Uniform Charlie Kilo Whiskey India Tango and then some,' he said while watching Prime Minister Bob Hawke on television.

He had two passions: making homemade mulled wine and ham radio operating. He had a shed in which sat a radio with a series of dials and illuminated panels that looked like it was out of an old adventure film.

He had, he told me, communicated with places across the globe, across the globe. And boasted that he could talk to farmers in Norway.

You could hear him yelling into the microphone from the backyard when he was competing against his sister-in-law's clapping. It sounded like some mad, meditative chant as he worked his way through the phonetic radio alphabet.

I asked my friend what her father talked about to his Nordic farming radio chums.

She didn't know but she said you always knew when he was talking to them because he got excited and yelled.

He was yelling now, so we supposed he was talking to them at that very moment.

'Does he speak Norwegian?' I asked my friend.

She said she didn't know but it sometimes sounded like it when he combined his ham radio operations with sampling his DIY alcoholic beverages.

But it was Trevor Tait's attitude towards his occupation which was the oddest thing about his behaviour, and when I was asked to fill in on a couple of Saturdays because Lenore and her 'idiot sister' were away with hockey carnivals I got a close-up view of the world of the holiday organiser.

It was very dark in the office and at first it wasn't that busy.

Mr Tait lifted up and answered phones that weren't ringing.

He rearranged a few posters and unwrapped some new catalogues.

Not much happened. We sat at desks. He with his big nameplate and me at Donna's as she didn't work Saturday.

'Well, time for a tea, time for tea – a Tango Echo Alpha,' said Mr Tait, and that seemed as good a time as any to chat to him.

I asked him what his favourite place was that he had been to on his own travels.

He almost snorted.

'Travel, no thanks, not me, not my cup of Tango Echo Alpha.'

I was a bit bewildered. 'You don't travel?'

He shook his head. 'Can't stand, can not stand it. Holidays at home, with the mulled wine and the radio, just at home are all I need.'

He was a travel agent but he didn't like travel and the only time he had travelled overseas was with the army to Malaysia. 'That was enough, let me tell you. Not much of anything there other than stuff that was different from what I liked. And the people were never really happy to see us and I mean, why would they be? Why would they be?'

He sat still for a moment and then said he had been on one holiday. With Lenore.

'Absolutely magnificent and it had Foxtrot Uniform Charlie Kilo all to do with bloody hockey. Absolutely magnificent.'

Where did he go?

'To Hobart.' He added, 'Tasmania,' just to make sure that I knew where it was.

'To Hobart?' I nearly laughed.

'Yes, yes, Hobart, Tasmania.' He smiled. 'To the opening of the Wrest Point Casino. Marvellous. Saw Jerry Lewis open the place and saw a prime minister of Australia, even if it was that clown Whitlam. Las Vegas down in the Southern Hemisphere. Then we played the pokies and saw a roulette wheel. A roulette wheel. Nothing like it since, so why try and top it?'

I must have looked a bit puzzled because he nodded his head and he explained that it wasn't his business to go on holidays; it was his business to get other people to go on their holidays.

He laughed. 'You know, William, you know, it's a bit of a gift to get somebody on a holiday. A gift. They come in here, the punters, and they have an idea of where they want to go and it's my job – my living – to get them off somewhere. Somewhere. Doesn't matter where, just as long as it turns a coin.'

He nodded. 'It's an art, an art.'

I was shocked to realise that he would get people on holidays at the best price to himself, even to the extent that he would attempt to actually talk people out of where they might like to go and point them in the direction of something similar but more unique and memorable.

Meaning more expensive, with a higher commission for him.

A young couple who came in were wondering about a holiday to French Polynesia. Trevor Tait nodded sagely then extravagantly gave his thoughts and opinion about where they really wanted to spend a holiday.

Apparently, it was a trip to Honolulu and then on to San Francisco. Amazingly, after a while, when he had shown the two holiday-seekers brochures and a few catalogues – swearing under his breath that the South Pacific catalogues borrowed by his youngest daughter hadn't been returned – he pointed out that going to French Polynesia meant that they would only see French Polynesians.

'You go to Honolulu and the other islands and you'll get the lot. You know, *The Brady Bunch*, *The Brady Bunch* – you remember that show? Well, they went to Hawaii and they had a ball.'

The young man looked a little nonplussed.

'And if you went to French Polynesia,' Trevor continued, 'you wouldn't see the USS *Arizona* memorial. That's the sort of thing you might like. And then you go to San Francisco. Much more to your liking.'

Amazingly they both thought that was a wonderful idea.

'And we mustn't forget the travel insurance, the travel insurance,' he said and he almost gave me a wink.

When the couple had left with their trip happily reorganised he almost whistled. 'Thank God for travel insurance, thank God. The commissions they pay.'

He pushed his luck occasionally and came a bit unstuck when he tried to convince an elderly Italian couple that instead of spending a month's holiday returning to the old country they might like to see Austria and Germany and he threw in a bus tour of a couple of places with odd names. When the couple both declared they didn't want to go to Austria or Germany or anywhere much else other than southern Italy, Trevor Tait audaciously claimed that he thought when they said 'the old country' they meant the 'unique Roman Empire tour, that went to those places that had once been a part of the lands that all the Caesars owned'.

The old couple left with a quote and Trevor said to me, 'Worth a crack, and you know a man has to eat, has to eat.'

A quirk of Trevor's was his way of answering the phone. I saw him pick up a phone that wasn't ringing a number of times and say into the mute receiver, 'Trevor Tait Travel, your holidays are my business.' He did this as quickly as he could in a series of three, each one a little faster and louder. Like a soldier presenting arms, thrusting his rifle out in front of himself, he would lift the phone, point it out in front like a lunging sword fencer, then grip the handpiece back to his head and speak.

He finally got to answer a phone call and put into practice what he had rehearsed. 'Hello, Trevor Tait Travel, your holidays are my business.'

He listened, gave a few 'hmms' of encouragement, then said solemnly, 'I'm so very, very sorry, very sorry to hear that.'

He told whomever it was to come down so that we could sort something out, and then when he hung up the phone he almost stood to attention.

'Absolutely bloody grand. They've had a recent bereavement and need to go on a holiday – a bloody gold seam has just run through this afternoon.'

Apparently there wasn't anything as good as punters wanting to get away on holiday to forget the awfulness that had befallen them.

'Sounded young too, that's even better,' said Mr Tait.

'What do you mean, Mr Tait?' I asked.

'Well, a young bereaved person wanting a holiday will throw cash around if they've got it, so it could be very, very good.'

It wasn't as if Mr Tait tried to stretch every customer for as much as they could spend; mostly he would attend to their requests. But, as he put it, 'When you feel there's a wind blowing, a wind blowing, what sort of sailor would you be not to try and fill the sails with it? And who knows where it will take you?'

He sat back down again under his kissing couple on board the sun-drenched cruise deck and ground his teeth. He drummed his hand on the desk and then banged it in delight.

'You never know, you never know, I might even get a chance to flog a holiday to Norway! To Norway!'

And he hummed as he went off to the kitchenette and made some International Roast coffee.

Mr Tait had a goal. A rather particular one but it seemed in keeping with the man – to try to sell a holiday to the land of the farmers he spoke to via his ham radio. 'Yes, the Kingdom of Norway, November Oscar Romeo Whiskey Alpha, Yankee – Norway.'

Why?

'Well, why not? Why not? Bit of fun. Bit of a challenge?'

'What's there in Norway to see? To do on a holiday?'

'What's to see in Norway? As far as I know, just a bunch of farmers who get on the turps. Tango Uniform Romeo

Papa Sierra. But some bugger out there might want to go.'
And he smiled.

'And a well-walleted youngster with a bit of grief under
their belt might be the go.'

A youngish man did come in later that afternoon and,
from where I was cleaning the kitchenette, I heard Trevor
Tait offer, 'the possibility of a cruise through the fjords of
the Kingdom of Norway might be the go'.

It didn't work out and the young man went with plans
for Hong Kong and Thailand.

Mr Tait stood staring wistfully as we locked up. 'Not
a bad day. Thought the young buck might have gone for
Norway for a moment.' He sucked in a deep breath. 'Well,
one day, one day.'

•

It wasn't long after Lenore and her sister came back from
'the bloody hockey thing' that I and a friend called Grunter
took off for a drive up the coast for the last weekend of the
uni holidays.

It didn't really make much difference that we took off late
on the Saturday night after a party was slowly fizzling out
and that all that was left of the last weekend of holidays was
the Sunday itself – we just thought it would be best to make
the most of what holiday time we had left to us.

Of course the car was ordinary, an old Chrysler that
Grunter had borrowed from his girlfriend's Uncle Ron, but
it seemed to chug along merrily enough. Driving it up the

highway was like being in a boat, the great square box gently going up and down, up and down, as we drove over all the cat's eyes there in the highway before us.

'The Valiant engine is a miracle, Willy, they just keep going,' said Grunter, who should have known what he was talking about seeing as he was an engineering student. 'They say the engine outlasts the car, that's why they went out of business.'

I nodded.

Then the car stopped.

The engine may have been okay but we forgot about something called petrol when we were sort of nowhere in particular. The car had stopped dead.

We were carefully prepared travellers with just a little less than the arse out of our pants and were as sensible as Burke and Wills. In the words of Trevor Tait, we were well and truly Foxtrot Uniform Charlie Kilo Echo Delta, Echo Delta.

'You got any money?' I asked Grunter.

'About as much as you.'

I laughed. Because I had nothing.

We walked a short distance and stopped. We didn't feel that great and we were lost.

That's when we heard the car. We turned and watched it drive up. We didn't wave; we just stood like stunned mullets. The car drove past us. It was a tiny car. A Hillman Minx. Unimaginably small. We didn't think the car would do what it did. It stopped. We watched it. It had stopped. Thinking. It puttered back.

Inside was a family of four. A man got out and smiled. He was dressed up. Well, he was wearing shorts, a shirt with a collar, long socks and desert boots. He was as dressed up as anybody had ever been by the looks of the bush around us, and he stood there smiling.

'Need a lift, boys?' he said.

We looked at each other and then we both nodded.

We wrenched ourselves into the little car. Everyone was smiling. A little like Donna when she was practising to be on *Sale of the Century*.

I sat next to a small boy who smiled at me like a character from the end of a Walt Disney film. Desperately appealing.

Grunter and I stank from what we had been recreationally imbibing.

'Where are you boys from?' asked the smiling mother.

'The uni,' gulped Grunter.

The smiling man who drove the groaning car had pushed his seat as far forward as it could go and was scrunched up against the wheel.

'Uni?'

'Yeah,' I said.

Grunter explained that we'd been at a party and decided to go for a bit of a drive during the holidays. And ran out of petrol.

'The uni,' muttered the man again, still smiling.

Another poor boy whose smile was becoming a toothy grimace said, 'Mummy, they stink.'

Nobody could argue with that.

The family was going to church and we were invited along to see what the pastor could do to help.

I remember that when we were presented to a clutch of men outside a small hall that was the church, Grunter was wearing a 'Never Mind the Bollocks It's the Sex Pistols' t-shirt.

The pastor was dressed almost exactly the same as the smiling man who had picked us up. Grunter had the sense to fold his arms over as much of the t-shirt as he could.

'Well, you're from the uni, are you?' said the pastor, and he made the word 'uni' sound like he was talking about a bad fart or dog shit on your boot.

We nodded.

'Uni.' He nodded. 'Well, we'll help you, of course. Our pleasure, we'll get some money for petrol and we'd love for you to join us for some lunch.'

Grunter liked that idea and went to shake the pastor's hand but remembered his t-shirt and quickly refolded his arms.

'Of course, we'd love for you to come and sit with us and worship.' All the men in shorts and long socks smiled at us and we smiled back and walked into the hall. It seemed the least we could do to repay their kindness.

Just before we were to sit, I took off my jacket and thrust it towards Grunter so he could cover his t-shirt.

'Good thinking, man,' he said.

So we sat in plastic-backed chairs and the worshipping began, and some songs were sung. The pastor read from the Bible and then he spoke about what he had read and it all sounded like somebody repeating a convoluted plot from some film at a barbecue when nobody is that interested.

'So it was when the rich guy died he thought it was all sorted but then the other, the poor guy, he ended up really having something that he never knew he had and then Satan, well, he's everywhere.'

Then he told a story about St Peter. Or Peter, as they called him.

I may have come from a family that my father described as 'advanced lapsed' but when they referred to 'Pete' I felt slightly uncomfortable. But then the night before caught up with me; I fell asleep.

Being woken suddenly is always a bit of a heart-starter but when it's somebody dragging you up a hall full of yelling people, who are surrounding you, it's quite a shock.

I yelled something unintelligible and was greeted with people yelling unintelligible things back at me.

Grunter gripped me. 'Come on, Will, come on, we got to get saved, we've got to get Jesus or they won't feed us.'

It was like being in a room full of Latin American soccer commentators celebrating a goal. I yelled again, Grunter yelled and the hall yelled.

We were pulled towards the front of the hall by helping hands belonging to the smiling men in shorts and long socks.

Standing at the front was the pastor, smiling and welcoming us to Jesus. He did this by placing his palm on the forehead of whoever was brought in front of him and then that person received Jesus.

It seemed that the best thing to do was to collapse like the woman in front of me had done and hope for the best.

'Just go with it, Willy,' said Grunter and he walked up, got a palm to the head and collapsed writhing on the floor.

I stared down at him in shock and then looked up at the smiling pastor. He looked at me and the smile disappeared. He stared at my chest. It was slightly disconcerting and then his eyes met mine with an odd look. He stepped towards me and said, 'Receive the power and glory of our friend, saviour and Lord, Jesus Christ.'

His surprisingly cold hand touched my forehead and I did the best receiving-Jesus collapse I could muster.

Next to me Grunter still writhed. He winked at me and whispered, 'It's okay, Willy, I'm just making sure they're going to feed me seconds as well as give me some petrol money.'

Later, as we ate a very nice lunch and Grunter helped himself to seconds and thirds, the pastor approached me.

He had the same odd look in his eyes and I hoped I wasn't going to have to receive Jesus again. I needn't have worried because he took another bite of a salad roll and pointed at my chest.

'That t-shirt of yours,' he said.

I glanced down at it. It should have been fine; I mean, Grunter was the one stuffing his face with a now proudly displayed 'Never Mind the Bollocks' effort. I was wearing a fairly harmless Trevor Tait Travel t-shirt that had been left over from a Central Queensland 'holiday expo' box that my hockey-playing friend thought might fit me.

I looked back at the pastor, who had a bit of shredded carrot on his lip, as he stared at me.

'Yes?' I said.

'That Trevor Tait fellow, he tried to sell me a tour to Norway when I was trying to book a flight to a Christian Living Conference in Auckland.'

He seemed to hold me responsible. He leant in closer. 'That man Tait is a mad bastard.' And then he almost smiled and the piece of shredded carrot rode on his lip. He winked. 'But his daughter, that Donna – not a bad-looking girl.'

I told Trevor Tait's hockey-playing daughter about this not long after and she roared with laughter and said that sounded like her dad.

We remained on pretty good terms but she soon started going out with a hockey player whom I think she later married.

Before she decided to let me down gently we had a sash-draping session in her and her sister's room. She went off to the toilet while I remained in a green Miss Sun Girl sash.

'I think this one suits me,' I said, turning, when I heard the door open. There before me in the doorway was her Aunt Denise, who had, true to form, walked into a room unannounced.

We stared at each other.

Then she smiled and clapped.

Then she disappeared.

I am pretty sure that she never told anybody because nobody ever said anything to me.

When my hockey-playing friend and I broke up I lost touch with the Taits, though I occasionally thought of Mr Tait when I heard the phonetic alphabet on some TV show or movie, and I couldn't help but laugh. Then, for no particular reason I could think of, a couple of years later I rang the travel agency on a Saturday and heard a familiar voice: 'Trevor Tait Travel, your holidays are my business.'

Then I said down the telephone line, 'I'm just enquiring about a holiday to Norway.'

There was a sharp intake of breath and I hung up.

Public Holidays

In the late 1980s when I was studying drama at the Western Australian Academy of Performing Arts (WAAPA) I had a job earning double time and a half stacking plastic chairs at a family fun day in Perth. I wasn't quite sure what the day was in aid of, but I had a feeling that it was something to do with the bicentennial. There was lots of talk about good Aussie tucker, which basically meant some guy in a big hat with a beard was cooking sausages and onions on a barbecue. It was very hot and there were lots of plastic chairs to stack and lots of families. And it seemed to me there was plenty of chaos to go around.

Children screamed, parents yelled, faces were painted, politicians spoke and someone who had the biggest, blondest perm, a not-so-current single 'in the charts' and wore a bright multi-coloured lycra outfit sang the national anthem. Or attempted to sing it; the sound system wasn't working properly so the singer's voice kept cutting in and out through the fuzzy hiss of the speakers.

Anybody who tried to do anything of an amplified nature sounded a little like the Norwegian farmers chatting to Trevor Tait in his shed.

It didn't really matter as nobody paid much attention to anything that went on upon the stage, which was festooned with little flags. It mattered even less when another man with a beard – a rather long and grand-looking beard – started speaking at a microphone and it sounded like the Norwegian farmers had become an alien from *Doctor Who*. Meanwhile a litany of names of lost children was called out in a drone by a woman who had tried to overcome the lack of a coherent PA system with the use of a loud-hailer.

One of my WAAPA classmates, who was also stacking plastic chairs, glanced across to me and indicated that I should have a gander at what was happening just behind me. I turned and saw a father standing there holding balloons and a clutch of giveaway show bags, with a simmering sooky look on his face while his wife shouted at him that, 'She didn't want to be a tiger, she wanted to be a zebra!'

A little girl beside them had tears running down the remnants of her tiger face, newly minted from the chaotic and undermanned face-painting stall.

'They were out of zebra paint . . .' sulked the father. A little boy holding the man's hand smiled in his zebra stripes.

'I got the last, I got the last!'

The mother said something but we never heard it.

The speakers suddenly began working and the bearded speaker's cry boomed out across the day, 'Families are what make the country we are, and they are a cornerstone of our society.'

The mother was giving the sulking father an almighty gob full of advice about parental responsibilities concerning face painting.

My friend looked to me and said, 'Willy, we're in trouble if that mob are a cornerstone.'

We laughed quite a bit, as I remember.

It was a Labour Day holiday, a holiday held to commemorate the granting of the eight-hour working day to Australians and to recognise the contributions to the economy by the nation's workers. That is what was printed on a pamphlet given out at a stall run by the Australian Council of Trade Unions.

I don't think our supervisor thought too much about the origins of the Labour Day holiday. He was a profoundly grumpy man and didn't seem to like the fact that two acting students were earning decent money from the hire company he worked for.

He thought we were 'pansies' who were 'taking a day's work off a normal person'.

He spat quite a lot when he spoke, especially when he got excited, and his disdain for us was enough to get him bothered. 'I could have rung up the talkback and got normal people who wanted to work, you know. I could have rung up.'

It turned out he was an assiduous listener to morning talkback radio. He continuously moaned about how we didn't know what hard work was and so, as a result, we didn't really appreciate the day off. 'You two don't know how to appreciate a public holiday, that's your trouble!'

'Now that's a bit harsh,' I said.

'You bloody don't, you've got to have a bloody job to appreciate a public holiday. Apparently you two are just pretend bloody actors.

'A public holiday is like an oasis in the desert of the working week, apparently – that's what they said on the talkback Friday morning,' our supervisor said. People like us 'apparently' took holidays for granted. 'Apparently' was a favourite word of his.

And apparently he was unhappy – 'I'm a bit cheesed off, I don't mind telling you pansies' – because there was no talkback today.

The routinely angry man who usually hosted talkback was off on holiday and so there was 'Just bloody music.'

He almost spat when he said again, 'Bloody music, apparently! And a holiday for what? Bloody unions. Too many bloody holidays.'

It was hard to keep up with his grumpiness but – apparently then, and funnily enough even today – listening to some of the ranting folk who occasionally populate talkback will have you believe we Australians get too many public holidays.

A uni lecturer of mine in a communications elective once said that people were basically unhappy and content to stay that way because having people tell them what to think from such low horizons of thought as talkback radio meant they didn't have to take responsibility for the opinions they spouted. It was enough to say 'The radio told me this or that'.

That uni lecturer ended up hosting a talkback radio show.

Nevertheless, I thought it might irritate our supervisor, Talkback, as I decided to name him, so I smiled and offered, 'You don't know that. You just operate on a low horizon of thought.'

He stared at me and then exploded in a spit fest. 'Bloody pansies – I'm complaining to the talkback!'

And he went back to the canvas tent he sat in; hard at work at whatever he was supervising. His role seemed to be to mumble and complain and occasionally speak into a walkie-talkie: 'Yep.' I don't suppose he was much of a supervisor really, only some poor shit-kicking bloke earning a dollar and having to put up with us 'pansies'.

Australia, as it turns out, doesn't even come close to having the most public holidays. China has the most and then there's India, Indonesia and a whole lot of others before Australia even registers.

But what Australians do – and here is where poor old Talkback was definitely wrong – is *appreciate* a public holiday.

Not for the reasons we have the public holiday, though. I doubt there were too many people at the family fun day who were thinking about the eight-hour day or the contributions of workers to the nation's wellbeing.

'People love a public holiday,' my classmate said. 'They might not give a rat's arse about why a public holiday is a public holiday, unless it's attached to a definite event, something like Anzac Day. You can't get away from the fact that a parade is a pretty big reminder!'

He laughed and looked over to where Talkback sat sulking in the tent. 'But they still love a public holiday – see how many punters are here today. They're all out and getting amongst it.

'We get creative with public holidays – we clump them together as much as we can to get a string of little breaks.'

It's true when you think about it. It's amazing just how many public holidays in Australia fall on a Monday, creating that little holiday subspecies known as the long weekend.

•

I thought of my classmate many years later when I was on my way over to Western Australia, again celebrating that convenient interlude of a weekend and a public holiday.

It was Lent and I was flying across the continent to the Perth Writers' Festival with three fourteen-year-old schoolgirls – my daughter and her two friends. I'd decided to try to give up swearing for Lent. Seemed like a good idea at the time: giving up swearing and taking the girls. Even the idea of Lent wasn't that bad.

The girls were great; it was me who was the problem. I have a propensity to be a grumpy middle-aged man prone to yelling. And swearing. Even during Lent. But I was not without a plan. I decided that while the odds of me actually getting through the whole process with my goal intact weren't great, I would attempt to substitute different words for my usual collection of oaths.

I strode through Melbourne airport, telling the girls to hurry so we would have enough time for me to have a watering stop.

'Look, if we hurry up I'll let you have some bar snacks and a Coke. How does that sound?'

'Excuse me, are you talking to me?'

I looked beside me. There was a woman waddling along next to me. No girls.

I apologised and said no, of course not.

She deadpanned back to me, 'Oh that's a shame, bar snacks would have been quite nice.'

It turned out the girls had stopped at a shop to look at something and hadn't told me. When I found them, I let them have it.

Well, in a manner.

I sounded like Chips Rafferty from some old black and white movie. ''Struth girls, you've got to tell me when you want to stop, you know. Crikey.'

They stared at me.

'Blow me down, I wanted a gargle. Fig jam.'

'Fig jam' was an expression I borrowed from a man who used to have a hardware shop down in Margate. I heard him use this oath when I was waiting to pay for some plaster of Paris and he was counting out some sharp little carpet tacks for another customer. He was a meticulous man and counted out the tacks loudly and clearly, probably as much for the benefit of the old lady who was buying the tacks as for himself.

All went well until he got to sixty-two and his metronomic counting stopped with a yell. I woke up from an almost hypnotic trance and the old lady dropped her bag of shopping. Two tacks had proven how sharp they were by getting caught under Mr Dyer's fingernail. He was, I could see, about to drop the f-bomb but stopped himself and said through gritted teeth, 'Fig jam, they're sharp.'

The girls, of course, were delighted to discover a new game: trying to make me break my vow in regards to the use of certain words.

On the plane I even trotted out 'great Caesar's ghost' when the man in front put his seat back a minute after take-off.

Nothing sounded quite right, and it struck me that the whole process was like the World Series Cricket crisis of the 1970s, when Australia lost all its top-shelf cricketers to Kerry Packer and had to substitute them with second-tier performers. So instead of a top-shelf player like Greg Chappell you got Graham Yallop. This metaphor amused me so I added Yallop to my list of stand-in curses for Lent. And I must admit, Yallop had a real ring to it, and he was a more than reasonable player who got burnt before he could really blossom.

Perth is, and always was in my memory, a comfortable city, with a beautiful river and lovely parks.

We stayed in a hotel down by the river with a landscape view. Unfortunately the view was a Jeffrey Smart landscape. All auto overpass, concrete and traffic signs. But the people at the hotel were nice and everywhere else was full.

Not just with the Perth Writers' Festival; there was a mining engineers' conference on as well. In fact, Perth being Perth, the mining conference was probably the main reason for the crowds. Checking in, we met two bemused men at the reception area engaged in a great Perth pastime: waiting for a taxi.

Waiting for a taxi in the town that likes to think of itself as the capital of the state that bankrolls Australia can be a pretty fraught experience. It's like waiting for some rare animal to show itself.

While there is some truth about Perth's importance to the national economy, with all the dirt dug up and shifted around in the north, no matter how much dirt is shifted it doesn't mean you'll be able to get a taxi when you want it.

One of the men was Scottish, the other American.

'You should have ordered a taxi a week ago,' I said.

'It doesn't take this long at home.' The Scot smiled.

The American shook his head.

'At home people don't get that upset over a cab,' he said.

They were bemused not only by the absence of taxis but also by the behaviour of another guest also waiting for a cab.

An Australian author, he was furious and foul-mouthed.

'Come on you f . . . ing c . . . of a thing.'

The Scot nodded. 'You Aussies don't know just how lucky you are.'

I shrugged. 'Maybe, but there's Yallopwits everywhere.'

'Yallopwits?' asked the American.

I pointed to the swearing guest and said, 'An Australian word for him.'

They nodded.

Germaine Greer opened the festival, talking about ecofeminism, slime moulds and Stephen Hawking. And even though she took a few cheap shots at Julie Bishop and Julia Gillard, and banged on about slime moulds as if nobody had ever noticed their worth, her speech was, at its heart, about respecting life. And whatever anybody may say, that is never a bad thing.

The girls thought the speech was okay but asked why she kept making the same point all the time.

'I think that's what happens at writers' festivals,' said my daughter.

'Fig jam!' I said. 'You're right there.'

•

The hotel had bicycles available for its guests so I promised the girls a ride around the Swan River bikeway. The bikes were like cabs – they didn't come.

Instead, we hired pedal cars that looked like the professor from *Gilligan's Island* had designed them. I barely fit but happily pedalled like a lunatic. The sun was shining and people were out and about, Perth-style.

Unfortunately, like every large Australian city, Perth is plagued by that small collection of certain exercisers who seem to think that public laneways are built for them and them alone.

A few angry men in lycra sped past us with a sneer and a non-Lent curse.

I heard my daughter laughing with her friends as their *Gilligan's Island* car wonkily made its way in and around the Sunday morning traffic.

Teenage girls' laughter on such a morning: it's a wonderful sound.

The girls yelled a collection of Lent, Chips Rafferty approved adjectives: 'Fig jam! You great Caesar's ghost!'

Another lycra curser zoomed past me and narrowly missed a man marching happily along. It was the Scottish engineer, taking a morning stroll. Before I could say anything, the Scot yelled out, 'Get knotted, ye Yallopwit!'

Now, for some reason, that made me feel very happy for Graham Yallop, a fine cricketer who never received his full due through a twist of fate; hopefully his name will go a bit global. Who says you can't learn something from Lent?

•

Sometimes though, a weekend won't be buttressed neatly against a public holiday because of the weird, floating cyclical nature of a calendar year. Some public holidays, like Anzac Day, have a set date — I mean what's the point of having Anzac Day on the 13th of December when the poor sods landed on the morning of the 25th of April?

And when the 25th of April falls on a Saturday or Sunday, in good old Australian fashion, and I'm sure much to the delight of the likes of Talkback, the holiday gets parked on the Monday.

But just why Easter always changes its dates is a mystery to me, though the head of movement at WAAPA tried to explain it to me once. She was a lovely lady with a great mournful face and an even greater ability to be patronising in an unintended way when people asked her things. This wasn't because she was rude or unpleasant, just that she was sure that she had a vast reservoir of knowledge about how the universe worked spiritually.

She was a great believer in 'the spiritual' and was endearing enough to claim that even a house brick has a spirit — you just have to know how to find it. One exercise she had us do was to hold a brick and try to connect with its spirit as we all sat around on a cold floor with our eyes closed listening to some wavering music.

One student, a rather intense man, said earnestly, 'This brick, I feel, has suffered but has known love.'

Well, good luck to him and the house brick.

It was after a movement class just before the Easter break that I asked a general question as to why the dates for Easter seemed to always change each year. My movement teacher gave a little half laugh and was joined by the intense man.

'Well, why do you think the dates change?' she said.

I said I didn't know, that was why I asked the question.

The intense man half laughed and smiled.

'Do you know?' I asked, looking to him.

The smile disappeared. 'No. I do not know.'

The movement teacher smiled and took a deep breath. She was about to impart some wisdom.

'It's because of the equinox, the vernal equinox.'

And she nodded.

I laughed. The equinox, moon and solar happenings were favourite words of hers and go-to answers for a multitude of questions. The traffic was bad on the Kwinana Freeway due to drivers being affected by 'the lunar cycle'. So too if somebody forgot their lines, wallet or underpants, 'the solar cycle'. The equinox was good for everything from stubbed toes to financial collapses and natural disasters.

Vernal equinox.

'That sounds like a Mormon elder from the Tabernacle Choir,' said another student.

'Or perhaps a singer who gets a solo,' offered someone else.

'Vernal Equinox,' said the intense man. 'Is he an actor?'

This made me laugh. Sir Vernal Equinox, a legend of the Victorian stage.

'No, no, no, no, no, no, no,' said the movement teacher and she paused and then said, 'no.'

Some holidays apparently are based around lunar and solar occurrences. Easter is one of those. 'It's on the first Sunday after the first full moon after the vernal equinox – the spring equinox of home —' the movement teacher laughed, 'I mean the northern hemisphere, and the equinox is when the night and day are of equal duration.'

She held her hands out from herself and then pushed them apart on the same level, as if she were smoothing down a tablecloth. 'So it's balanced, a very balanced time. A special time. There's a beautiful light about. A spiritual light.'

Well, it was as good an explanation as any we were going to hear and it certainly satisfied the intense man, whom we soon christened Vernal.

'So that is why there was the light, the special light when Jesus was crucified?' He sounded like a character trying to piece together a mystery on a bad television show.

The mournful movement teacher stared at him. Vernal looked unsure.

'A beautiful light, a spiritual light, and a man on a cross dying for his people? Very dramatic,' said Vernal.

The mournful teacher smiled.

'Well, I'm sure that would make the poor fellow think it was all worth it. Yes, the theatre of religion.'

Vernal blinked. Nobody knew whether the mournful movement teacher was having a go or just speaking nonsense. Maybe she was doing both.

•

It made me think of a week squashed together and compressed by the Mormon elder Vernal Equinox back in 1973.

Easter Monday was on the 23rd and Anzac Day was the Wednesday of the same week. I remember that Easter because of a comment I heard after the Thursday religious instruction lesson had finished and we were on our way to little lunch.

It was made by a teacher called Mr Stuart, a tall man with a beard who was a very good rugby player and, astoundingly, at least to me, popular amongst his students.

He was also a fairly good golfer, who would take the great T-square school ruler and practise a few drives with it and then say to some of the more unruly boys in his class, 'How would you like that across your backsides?'

Then he would say, 'More wood for a longer drive.' To make sure everyone in the class understood who was boss.

So when he pointed to me and a few of my friends and said, 'That lot?' as he chatted to some other teachers and the elderly woman who had just taken religious instruction, I knew we were for it.

'You three come into my room for a little talk.' And he grabbed the big wooden T-square ruler.

This talk I knew was because of what had transpired in religious instruction when the elderly lady had asked the usual questions about this time of year.

'Why do we celebrate Easter?'

'Jesus died on the Cross,' was a rote answer from a few kids in the class who played along. The idea of celebrating a person dying on a cross seemed sort of strange, even though you knew what was coming next.

'And he rose again on the Sunday? Why?' said the elderly lady. 'Why did Jesus rise again?'

It had been a dry, warm April and that made it so easy to zone out and drift away, especially when some poor old thing was banging on about a story everybody knew. And now she was banging on again about Easter, not just a holiday but also a special time. I realised she was asking me.

'Why had he risen again? Why had he woken up?'

The way the elderly lady spoke, it was as if Jesus had forgotten to do something.

And I could think of no reason – why would anybody wake up? Why would I wake up? Who did I know who would wake up and, from the way the elderly lady was putting it, seem to have forgotten something?

My father. I thought of my father. 'Oh Christ, the bloody bins,' and he would haul himself out of bed and rumble down the stairs to put the rubbish bins out for early morning collection.

Why did he rise again?

'To put the bins out,' I said. 'Or to do wees.'

The two boys next to me laughed till snot ran out of their noses.

I apologised as quickly as I could and the elderly lady

looked at me 'more in disappointment' and mumbled, 'That's a silly thing to say.'

We really should have been packed off to see Stevo but Mr Stuart took us in for the little chat and he stood swinging the T-square.

'You think it's funny to be rude to a person about what they believe?'

We stared at him.

And he practised his swing some more.

I said, 'No, sir.'

The other two boys were allowed to go. He swung the T-square ruler again.

'So Christ rose to put the bins out?' said Mr Stuart, and I sort of thought he almost smiled. He checked his grip on the T-square and looked at me. 'When you learn a bit about life and see what sort of courage it takes to even think about sacrifice then maybe you can laugh at people's stories. But grow up a bit first and go say sorry again.'

And he swung the T-square ruler with great force just to one side of me.

'Yes, straight down the middle.'

I did as I was told and the elderly woman nodded her head and gave me a light tap on the shoulder.

•

The Easter in 1973 was an odd holiday weekend. It seemed to roll along evenly enough. On Good Friday I let Jesus do his thing on the Cross and tried not to think of Mr Stuart, and on the Saturday morning I awoke to hear my mum and dad banging on about what was in the *Courier-Mail*.

They were talking about something called abortion. There were stories of how a private member's bill was being presented to the federal parliament to provide abortion on request for the first fourteen weeks of pregnancy.

'It's just a lot of old men telling women what they should and shouldn't do with themselves,' said my mother. 'It's about time women could sort it out for themselves.'

My father grunted. 'Well, there's always going to be silly old men telling all sorts of people what to do with themselves but they should put a sock in it.'

I asked what abortion was.

My father shook his head.

All my mother said was, 'Something nobody ever takes lightly – except people who want to boss other folk around.'

All I could think of was my teachers.

'Well, things are changing all right,' said my father and he pushed me out into the day with my mother yelling after me, 'Your job is not to turn into silly men who tell people what to do!'

On Monday I went for a walk along the beach in the early morning and saw an old man in a great straw hat catch a couple of flathead.

The bay was like a mirror.

As he pulled a fish from the water, its efforts of resistance were half-hearted, almost as if it didn't realise it was a matter of life or death for itself. Well, it was just a fish.

Later that day we went to Lang Park to the rugby league match between Redcliffe and Wests and to everyone's stunned amazement Redcliffe thrashed them in a boilover, 27 to 2.

There were head-high tackles and biffo from both sides, and even an attempted conversion by a Redcliffe player called Merv Cook that went to poo when, after what seemed an age, he'd carefully sculpted his little mound of sand and placed the ball just so and then solemnly stepped back to kick the ball, only to toe-poke the ground and nearly break his foot.

As he limped back, another Redcliffe player called Ian Thinee laughed so much he nearly dropped the ball from a kick-off.

'They would have beaten anyone today,' said my father as we drove home. 'Anyone.'

The next day I wanted to read what the *Courier-Mail* said about the Redcliffe Dolphins, but on the front page there was other news from Redcliffe.

There had been a boating accident just off the Scarborough reef, two boats had capsized and a woman had drowned.

For two hours a man had held onto the woman, his wife, by clinging to a reef marker; holding her up above the water in an attempt to save her life.

Holding her even after he knew she was probably dead.

I looked at the photo of the reef on the front of the paper, with arrows indicating where people had been. There were photos of two young men who had dived in to try to help.

I read the paper and thought about how I had been at the football, having a holiday, laughing at Merv Cook's kick like

Ian Thinee had, while this man had held his dying wife in his arms for hours.

I read the riotous coverage of the Redcliffe Dolphins' victory from the craggy old football writer Jack Reardon with the immortal lines, 'Referee Bernie Pramberg penalised Redcliffe Captain Ron Raper three times for high tackles and perhaps he may have gone a bit too far. At worst Raper was a bit over-vigorous.' I laughed but still couldn't be quite at ease with what had happened over that holiday.

I saw Mr Stuart at little lunch at school and thought perhaps I should try to tell him that maybe I understood a little of what he had said about life and sacrifice. How things seemed so unfair.

But all the kids wanted to do was talk to him about the footy and how 'we' had thumped Wests.

I walked away and I suppose I forgot, but those holidays were never the same.

•

The next day during the Anzac march all the old men who wobbled along didn't seem so old and wobbly. But I don't think I could put my thoughts into any perspective until I was much older.

Sometimes when you look beyond the time-off aspect, the meaning of some public holidays can give you a reason to think about certain aspects of a life.

Like Anzac Day. Lives from another time, another era, when Australia was barely past colony status. Young men who muddled ashore and fought through the horrors of that Dardanelles campaign – a grand design by a great man of history called Churchill – most likely considered themselves to be Britons.

They fought in the name of an English king. Patriotic duty. They fought for an idea of freedom. Whether that sacrifice was justified or not may never be known.

But the worth of that sacrifice has lessons. One of the most significant for me is that upon those headlands of Turkey the idea of worth as an Australian was made abundantly clear.

It didn't matter the cut of your cloth, the colour of your school tie, the amount of your bank account, your class – it was the willingness to shed your blood. To give your life alongside your compatriots.

I have no comprehension of what that sacrifice must be like. Maybe it's just a myth – but it's a powerful one.

Sometimes when I see Anzac Day tarted up to decorate a football match, an advertising campaign or add lustre to a politician's sheen, I grow tired.

Sacrifice. My father told me he wasn't that sure about God but God's son was the best the top shelf had to offer. Although my family was 'advanced lapsed', Good Friday and the story of that Nazarene's sacrifice on behalf of his people have always been powerful to me.

Where he got the strength, the faith, to do what he did, I never have been able to fathom. Even if it's just that, a story, then it's a mighty story of generosity, compassion, courage and belief. There are worse things to try to live by than the words of a man who cared so much for people.

Easter, and especially Good Friday, is the earning of the joy of Christmas.

And everybody loves a celebration.

Sometimes, when I think about what the Anzacs, and the succeeding generations of Australian servicemen and women, fought and fight for, I don't think it's got much to do with the proposition that a person born into a particular family is worth more and is deserving of more adulation than one born in the poorest street, in the shabbiest town.

Anyone for a story about a king born in a manger?

•

What my plastic chair stacking mate would have made of the Melbourne Cup holiday is anyone's guess, because there isn't much point to it other than a holiday for a holiday's sake. There are plenty of signs it's Melbourne Cup time – roses bloom, the sun shows spring is well and truly under way, then storms sweep in from nowhere to drench the city and disappear just as quickly, and photos of Bart Cummings appear with alarming regularity throughout every newspaper.

The first Tuesday in November isn't affected by any lunar or solar events, nor by the equinox – which almost sounds like a horse that might be running in the Cup. And the Monday is magically grafted on to the Tuesday by schools and businesses to produce the Spring Carnival long weekend.

There are also sure hints it's Cup time in shop windows. The local hairdresser has a sign: 'Get your fake tan for the Spring Racing carnival!' While two shops down, the op shop has 'Melbourne Cup suits!' These things look like something Bob Menzies wore to a messy breakfast. The concept of mixing Sir Robert Menzies with a fake tan is a tad disconcerting but it's pleasant knowing Cup time is near.

The Melbourne Cup makes me think of many things: women wearing teetering high heels and tiny dresses, and young men wearing tight suits and little hats, all mostly full of grog, mostly wasted and bedraggled. They'd also be good names for stablemate racehorses. Wasted and Bedraggled. Give Bart a call.

It makes me think of the marquee area – where people sit to be seen or get giddy on free fizz and burp on the canapés.

And then there's Larry Pratt.

You can't make up a name like that. Larry Pratt was Brisbane's ABC racing commentator for years and had a politely apologetic air about him. His great tradition was the Cup morning phantom call, where he'd call the race as he divined it. It was always played a bit before eight and was a part of my life for years. Larry's claim to fame was being the only pundit to back Baghdad Note, a noble grey, to win the Cup in 1970.

It was because of this mighty feat of judgement that my father hung on to his faith in Larry when many others used far trustier methods of picking a winner, like reading chicken entrails or consulting a cross-eyed astrologist.

'This bloke knows his stuff – picked Baghdad Note, don't you know!' was uttered by Dad the first week of every November for years. Larry, like any trackside Nostradamus, could be a bit hit and miss and just as some doubt set in, he came up with Dulcify in 1979 – only to be failed by the tragic champion's breakdown.

This gave renewed hope to my father. 'You see – it would have won but it didn't,' was his justification for upholding the Pratt faith.

One morning, enough was enough. Dad snorted as Larry 'phantomed' away. 'Might as well pick bloody Francis the talking mule as soon as anything.'

People say the Melbourne Cup is lots of things, tarting it up for no good reason other than to sell something.

Frippery and frills can masquerade indulgence and desperate betting but to me – at its heart – the Cup has always been fun. Especially so when you take the chance to make use of the long weekend down at the beach with your daughter. And three of her schoolmates. And Thor and Wolverine.

The girls and I were bunched around the telly – in between trips to the beach and bushwalking – watching a whole lot of attractive men with huge chins and muscles, as well as other less muscled characters who did nothing much except meet an exotically grisly end. After four days I felt immersed in the inner circle of the Big-Chinned Ones.

Apparently the whole idea of having a superhero movie festival was born out of a school lunchtime discussion of literature and, in particular, *Pride and Prejudice*.

I have no idea how this occurred but I'm sure there's a lineal progression from Jane Austen to Thor and the rest of the big chins.

The girls awarded points for who was the best superhero; Thor and Spider-Man came out on top. Chris Hemsworth would be the sporty superhero you would take to a junior formal. Tobey Maguire was the smart, cute nerd you would talk to at the formal while Chris was off talking footy with the superhero jocks.

The girls start giving people assorted doppelgängers, so the odd Maths teacher from their school was superhero Magneto from *X-Men*, the bald guy from the same movie sounded like a droning bishop, and the nasty traitor from *Salt* had eyes like someone's big brother.

What I wasn't prepared for was just how much silly mayhem and nonsense fourteen-year-old girls could enjoy.

And it was interesting to watch the way the girls understood irony, adding bucketfuls of their own.

When Captain America was transformed from a skinny computer-generated geek into a beefy big-chinned guy in a rather questionable outfit, all with the aid of chemical enhancement, one of the girls mentioned that perhaps the good captain was the Lance Armstrong of superheroes.

'You know, he's topping himself up with performing-enhancing . . . things.'

'So do you drug test superheroes?' I asked.

Well, there would be no point, they decided, because, 'It's like the cycling or the Olympics. Everyone would be doing it.'

'And the whole point of superheroes is that they're super and if they don't take something then some random accident injects them with something anyway.'

There was a pause and then another asked, 'But would the good deeds of a superhero who used perform-enhancing things not count?'

'Perhaps the end justifies the means.'

'That's a question that opens up all sorts of issues.'

'That sounds like something that that Julian Assange might say. He sounds like he should be in a superhero movie with a name like that.'

'He thinks he *is* in a superhero movie and he's the hero,' I said.

My daughter told me that I should stop being such a COF (Conservative Old Fart).

I smiled, for her mother used to call me that when she wanted to tease me.

My daughter looked at me and said, 'Dad, if you were in a superhero movie you'd be . . .' She paused.

'Thor?' I said. No, those days are long gone.

'Maybe Odin, Thor's old man.'

There were a few dismissive giggles.

All of a sudden I was interested. 'Who would I be, really?'

Probably someone who yells, I was told, like Spider-man's editor or a grumpy general. Or the bad guy with the eyebrows, or that nasty president.

Great.

No superhero status, but it's okay. The girls, inspired by the big-chinned heroics and daredevil behaviour, decided it was time for a break and headed down to the beach.

Amazingly, despite the rain that swept across the shallow bay they decided it was time for a swim too. Why not? It's a superhero long weekend.

They all shivered, howling and screaming in delight at the rain and the coldness of the seawater.

Then somebody pointed across the bay to the Nobbies and Phillip Island.

'Isn't that where Thor lives?'

Thor?

'Well, his family – where he grew up.'

Phillip Island?

'Yeah, that's where he and his little brother grew up.'

'His little brother is a bit wet.'

'Well, I like him.'

'I like Thor better.'

'Everyone likes Thor – go Chris!'

The girls in a shivering clutch decide to sing to Thor and his little brother. They did an impromptu version of their school song, which is about a Jesuit nun, and added in a few shimmies and non-nun movements.

Then they all howled in laughter and splashed in the water and I thought how could you not enjoy the sheer lovely nonsense of them all?

I suddenly thought of Talkback and his moaning about public holidays we don't need.

I suppose he was the sort of man my mother had warned me about turning into.

A silly man who spent his time telling other people what to do with themselves.

And I thought of that family day public holiday when he moaned at us 'pansies' and then hid in his little canvas supervisor's tent, and how I could never have imagined myself doing anything else other than stacking chairs. But I ended up with a family of my own and here on that windy beach, as my daughter and her friends laughed and sang out to Thor, I thought how could I better spend a public holiday?

'Oh shut up, Talkback, you poor old sod,' I said to the wind and myself.

Hit and Run Holidays

'It'll be a hit and run holiday – we get in, see the pussycats and get on home. Over to Africa and back in a day. Bob's your uncle,' Mr Muff said to my father.

My father wasn't too sure. 'It's a long way, Brian, you might be pushing it.'

Brian Muff, father of Darren Muff, was of the opinion he could get down to Beenleigh and see the Bullen's African Lion Safari Park, have a birthday picnic and get back to Redcliffe in a day.

It was Darren's birthday and Brian Muff, who worked in flooring sales, was a can-do man.

'We'll be right – a hit and run holiday.'

There were seven of us in the Muff family's Hillman Hunter and we set off for the safari. It might have been a suitable name for a vehicle going off on a safari – the Hillman Hunter – but it was one of those too-cosy English cars masquerading as a family sedan. An English family sedan in which there was barely space to breathe, let alone any wriggle room. And there wasn't a seatbelt amongst us.

It was a clean car, though, with a little plastic dog with a bobbing head on the panel behind the back seat, and the whole car smelt very sweet. At first it was like a smell of lollies and we all laughed and tried to work out what lollies they might be.

'Fruit tingles.'

'Jujubes.'

'Raspberries.'

'Musk sticks.'

We chugged along in high spirits and wondered how many lions we might see prowling on the safari.

'There's not just lions, you know,' said Mr Muff. 'There's all number of jungle beasts.'

'Tigers?' asked Darren.

'No, not tigers, not an African animal, common enough mistake to make. They're from India.'

'Elephants? Are there elephants?' said another boy.

'My word, there'll be elephants, though they'll be Indian ones.'

'If they have Indian elephants, why don't they have tigers?'

asked Darren Muff, who was riding shotgun in the front seat with his father.

There was a pause and I think that's when the hit and run holiday hit a snag. The lolly smell became suddenly sickly and Mr Muff snapped, 'Shut up, Darren.'

The space seemed to constrict us even further and a boy called John King started saying he couldn't breathe properly so we opened a window and then the little dog's head started shaking up and down as if it was having a fit. Mr Muff told us to wind the window up.

And that is how we spent most of the hit and run holiday, being pressed together for hours on end while Darren Muff sobbed in front.

When we got to Bullen's African Lion Safari Park we drove through some gates and around to the picnic tables not far from the kiosk and the toilets. All these building were decorated with a vaguely African safari trim but other- wise it looked a little like we were locked in a big tennis court-cum-birdcage.

There seemed to be heaps of these theme lands back in the seventies and eighties, where somebody had an idea of building a 'tourist holiday attraction'. Almost as if there was a series of mum and dad small business people who had a bit of a Walt Disney complex. My father called them Ma and Pa Kettle outfits after the old comedy film characters from the 1950s.

There was Adventure Land at Samford, which was like a big garage of horse-drawn coaches with a 'lake' you paddled canoes on. In truth, it was like a big farm dam but it was better than Lone Pine, where the highlight was to have your photo taken with a stonkered koala.

Santa Land down at the Gold Coast was too weird for words and, of course, there was the Big Cow and Big Pineapple at the other end of the coast.

And on the Sunshine Coast was another strange attraction. My mother took us one holiday; it was a replica of the *Endeavour*, Cook's ship on his voyage of discovery.

It was half finished, very orange and was run by a fit but odd Englishman who showed us around the boat in ten minutes. His wife appeared from nowhere and offered us a Captain Cook Devonshire tea, the cream of which came out of a tube, which looked like No More Gaps. Then we went home.

'No wonder they all got scurvy,' said my mother.

It was very odd but I guess they were just people having a go at the holiday attraction business.

Bullen's seemed to be a holiday attraction that was a little more epic.

The safari park, which played on the popularity of films such as *Born Free* and *Living Free*, was designed to bring the wilds of the African plains to scrubby bits of Australian semi-rural bush.

It must have been a town planner's dream because no sooner had the park been built than housing began to pop up around it.

The safari park's owners got a knacker's licence so they could butcher injured horses for the 'jungle beasts of Beenleigh' and even went so far as to put an advertisement in a local paper: 'Free livestock removal service. Sick or injured cows and horses removed promptly, free of charge. Phone Bullen's Lion Park.'

An elephant escaped once, was found wading happily through some rubbish heaps and had to be coaxed back into the park by handlers talking in an Indian accent because the elephant had been trained in India and only responded to that accent.

Still, bad Peter Sellers accents apart, the safari park was the home of big cats and rogue elephants, and also the remnants of Bullen's Circus.

Bullen's was the circus that my head full of perm inspired the Maths teacher and sports master to nickname me after.

Given that was over a decade after the circus folded they must have had long memories, or perhaps been jolted by a similar trip to the lion safari.

All the leftover circus animals seemed to have been sent to the different safari parks around Australia to thrill carloads of visitors.

And here was another snag. The Hillman Hunter.

It was decided, by Mr Muff, that as the trip down had taken so long we should save time and have presents and the birthday cake first, and then perhaps eat the picnic on the go so we could get a 'good look-see' at the beasts of the jungle and Beenleigh from the vast interior of the Hillman Not-so-big-game Hunter.

No sooner had we untangled ourselves and rushed cake and cordial down our throats, sung a fairly muted round of 'Happy Birthday' and thrown presents to Darren – he got two bug catchers, which was a tad embarrassing for a boy of nearly ten – than we were ordered off to the toilet block and then back into the car.

The toilet block, I remember, stank of bleach but we stayed long enough to have a pissing contest up the urinal wall and the winner howled Tarzan-like in delight. Then back into the Hillman Hunter with sandwiches thrust at us to eat as we groaned around the compound.

'Keep the windows wound up' was the advice from a few signs and so Mr Muff decided it was better to be safe than sorry. 'These things can turn, you know – they are wild animals.' He shifted in his seat to wind up the driver's-side window.

Everybody knew that the cracking sound that came from the front seat wasn't going to be good but perhaps Darren could have waited till later to point out to his father what had happened.

Darren whined, 'My bug catcher – you broke it.'

There was a pause, silence and then Mr Muff said tartly, 'Shut up, Darren.'

'All windows up, boys' was the order and the Hillman Hunter closed itself for the business end of the lion safari and we crawled away.

It was a hot day in the era before air conditioning was a given in every car, so the atmosphere of genuine fear of wild animals that could turn, the disappointment of a broken bug catcher, and the percolating aromas of the egg sangers, and ham and cheese and pickle, and lolly party bags began to be quite toxic.

The little plastic dog's head bobbed up and down almost as if it was about to be sick.

We parked in a semicircle where other cars were gathered.

It was unbearably sticky and hot.

'Lions!' cried Darren.

We turned, or rather tried to because it was like one heaving mass of limbs and thongs and sandwiches.

We saw sandy logs lying about in a bit of a clump. Lions. They were snoozing like nobody's business.

'Windows up!' snapped Mr Muff. The windows were up.

A Land Cruiser painted in zebra stripes and pulling a man in a cage rolled passed us. The man lazily pushed lumps of meat out of small flaps and suddenly from nowhere, the lions got up and ambled over for a feed.

The size of them was a shock; even though they seemed medicated, they were impressive.

'He's after the man!' cried Mr Muff. We were unsure, how could a lion get at a man in a cage? We thought he was trying to gee us up but he was an adult. It was the way he said 'man'. Like he added a couple of syllables that weren't needed. Then he beeped the horn. That was the real giveaway he was serious.

One of the creatures turned its head towards us for a few seconds.

There was silence in the car.

'The lion's on the cage!' said Mr Muff.

'They're feeding it,' said Darren.

Mr Muff was about to say something, when one of the lions let out a roar and the whole car erupted, led by Mr Muff.

'Windows up! Windows up!'

Mr Muff, I saw, was holding an egg sandwich and every time he yelled he squashed it more.

'Windows up!'

The man in the cage didn't seem too fazed and there were a few khaki-clad safari people around who looked bemused.

The lions went about their business and we groaned through the rest of the compound. When we came to another gated section called 'bushland menagerie' we weren't so much like a Hillman Hunter but an overstocked Swedish Sauna. A boy asked if he could wind the windows down, and Mr Muff agreed hesitatingly.

'There's no lions, Dad,' Darren said with a certain tone, 'or do you want to beep your horn?'

Mr Muff wound down the window and raised an egg sandwich he had almost squashed into an elongated relay baton and turned to his son. 'Beep my horn? Shut up, Dar—'

He'd wound his window down a little further than he meant to, and I think just how the donkey liked it.

I never knew donkeys were a part of the bushland menagerie but this one looked happy enough. And why wouldn't he? He obviously liked elongated egg sandwiches.

He nibbled at the sandwich the way Mr Ed the talking horse used to move his lips, which was sort of interesting.

I don't know if Mr Muff ever watched *Mr Ed* but when the donkey murdered the egg sandwich, Mr Muff turned the second part of his son's name into an elongated scream. So 'Shut up, Darren' became 'Shut up, DaRRRRRAAAAA! Windows up! Windows, windows UP!'

I can't remember how long it took for us to stop laughing. But when we did, we drove back to Redcliffe. We didn't even get time at the kiosk. It took even longer because there was a breakdown on the Hornibrook Bridge.

Spot fires of sniggering would break out and then be dampened down by a glowering Mr Muff but trying not to laugh made it all the harder and more delightful when it happened.

When I got home, my father asked me how it was, and I told him a donkey had bitten Mr Muff.

My father laughed. 'Wild Kingdom eat your heart out! A hit and run holiday!'

•

The term 'hit and run holiday' branded itself in my mind as a fitting description of a quick holiday away that was often accompanied by some panic and a slight careering off course.

This doesn't mean the whole H and R holiday goes down the drain and is as wildly entertaining as our trip to the wilds of Beenleigh; it's just that things seem to happen on H and R holidays.

Like my holiday to Mildura where, as with all great H and R efforts, we just jumped and went. It turned out to be a couple of days away with a sparse wardrobe and a pretty eager stomach.

Mildura, in northwestern Victoria, has heaps of fruit growers and lots of lovely paddle-steamers paddling along the Murray River. There's an old hotel on the riverbank called the Grand.

And in this lovely old hotel is a restaurant called Stefano's that specialises in degustation.

If you ask someone who knows about such things, degustation is basically a culinary experience where the diner sets out to taste and savour the signature dishes of a particular chef.

Many courses are presented in miniature and there's an accompanying wine menu to match. When savouring a food, its taste, aroma and presentation seem to be as important as actually eating it.

To put degustation in boofhead terms, it's like a top-shelf hamburger with the lot or a chock-full, 'the works' pizza.

The best way to describe degustation though is to think of eating in terms of cricket. A normal meal out is like a game of one-day cricket. A sly piece of junk food purchased from a drive-through and consumed in the bubble of your own car is like a Twenty20 fixture. Degustation is like a

Test match. On and on it goes, with a never-ending stream of merry drinks breaks.

We had a ludicrously young English wine waiter who knew way too much about the wine. He was like an encyclopedic vino spruiker and had more patter lines than Dennis Cometti, the Aussie Rules commentator. 'If merlot was a dog it'd be a Labrador. Pleasant, boring and a little smelly.'

'Why doesn't anybody like merlot?' I asked.

The young waiter smiled. 'Because,' he paused for effect, 'it's merlot.' His next recommendation was a bit of a stretch. It was a shiraz, or 'a shirazza!' as one member of our dining party called it.

The young waiter smiled again and then suggested, 'No, not a shirazza, more of a Jane Bennet.'

The shirazza mutterer asked, 'What, as in *Pride and Prejudice*?'

The young waiter nodded.

'Yes, the eldest Bennet girl and you must think of yourself as Mr Bingley.

'This wine is like that person you should marry – it's there waiting to be asked, yet you just don't see it. The perfect partner, shy but beautiful, just waiting for you to propose.'

He would have been past twenty if he was lucky but his barefaced cheek was so entertaining.

'So why not all be Mr Bingley and get down on bended knee?'

The dessert was richer than Rupert Murdoch and, just like dear old Rupert, it was everywhere. Including on my shirt. I'd only brought two with me.

Never mind, I was told that there was a laundry in the hotel.

•

Degustation wasn't the only thing Mildura had to offer.

One of the local attractions, imaginatively called Orange World, is one of those Ma and Pa Kettle efforts that have survived the demise of all those other Walt Disney would-bes of the 1970s. Orange World was set on, of all places, an orange farm, and had a tractor pulling orange-shaped carriages through the groves of the orchard.

Inside the kiosk there was a multitude of orange-themed things to buy. I picked up an oddly shaped plastic green thing and said to a friend, 'Look, this thing shouldn't be here. It's not orange – it's green.'

The proprietor, a lovely man called Mario, approached me and delicately took the non-orange green thing from my hands and said, 'This, this is my favourite of all Orange World's attractions.'

I looked at him and he smiled and picked up an orange.

He held it up. 'An orange.'

I nodded.

He held up the non-orange green thing.

'An orange peeler – look!'

He popped the top of the peeler into the orange and rotated the orange and the skin came off.

I love something that looks like it makes something easy and I immediately bought one.

'You know, the great thing about the peeler is that it takes off the whole skin in one piece.' Mario smiled.

'Yes, I can see that,' I said.

'It is easy and convenient to dispose of.' He picked the orange peel up. 'And it is perfect to find the one you love!' He winked, held the peel above his head, twirled it around three times and threw it down on the floor.

'What letter did it make?' We both bent down to peer at the orange peel on the floor.

'Ah, I see you know this game,' said Mario.

I nodded. 'Used to play it at school.'

The idea is that the shape the orange peel makes when it lands is the first letter of the name of the person you love.

We looked at the peel.

'S,' I said.

Mario agreed. 'Susan!'

'Is that who you love?'

'My wife's name is Domenici.'

'Then the peel's got it wrong?'

Mario smiled. 'Not necessarily.'

I picked up an orange and tried to peel it. Like anything, there was a knack to actually using the peeler effectively and it didn't work nearly as easily as it did for Mario. I botched it and the peel broke. I looked to Mario. He nodded to take another.

The non-orange green thing that is the orange peeler is a hard beast to master. I slaughtered another orange.

I looked to Mario. He shook his head. No more oranges.

My shirt was now covered in mangled orange.

Never mind, I told myself, there's a laundry in the hotel.

'Do you think that the peel ever makes anything other than an S?' I asked by way of making conversation.

Mario thought and nodded. 'I have never seen the peel ever give anything other than an S. We all have our own tastes – the peel likes S!' He shrugged his shoulders and smiled. 'It is a marvellous gift, this orange peeler. Use it well!'

I assured him that I would. And then Mario said, 'I have seen you somewhere before, haven't I? You aren't on the television, are you?'

I admitted I'd occasionally been seen on television screens.

Col, a tourist coach driver who had just dropped off a busload of people to be driven through the groves in orange carriages, snapped his figures and pointed at me like a television lawyer pointing at the accused in court.

'You're that bloke that sells things.'

I stared back.

'Like what?'

'Those steak knives and things. Vegie cutters, all that crap.' He picked up one of Mario's non-orange green orange peelers.

'Yeah, this sort of crap!'

Mario smiled and nodded. 'You,' he said, also pointing at me. 'You are Tim . . . Shaw.'

What to do? Do I say, 'Mario and Col, I'm a fat old ham who scribbles a bit,' or do I just smile and say, 'Wait, there's more'?

Well, there's always more.

'Hey!' said Mario. 'Didn't you run for the Senate for the Liberals?'

'Did I?'

'You didn't get anywhere – but you had a go.'

At least Mario smiled.

•

I have been mistaken for all sorts. I was recognised as Colin Firth, of all people, in Canberra by a senator, much to the incredulous delight of my daughter. All I can say is it must have been a good night at the Members' bar.

On a tram going to a festival I was approached by a young man with a neatly sculpted beard – we were heading to St Kilda and I cursed myself that I hadn't packed a beard. He half smiled and walked a few steps to where I hung onto a strap.

'You are who I think you are, aren't you?'

'Well, who do you think I might be?'

I shouldn't have asked.

'Mark Latham,' said the sculpted beard. The volcanic former leader of the Labor Party. The man with the sculpted beard smiled and nodded, 'You're Mark Latham. Way to go, you.'

I stared at him. Way to go.

I couldn't do anything else other than nod.

As we stepped off the tram the sculpted beard gave me the thumbs up and I nodded in my best Mark Latham manner while my daughter said with a straight face, 'I liked it better, Dad, when you were Colin Firth.'

But back to Mildura. The Demtel Man? I should have known that it could only get better.

I sat on a paddle-steamer that was making its way to a winery and a man in uniform was glancing at me every now and then. I nodded a few times and he looked blankly back.

He seemed to do a bit of everything, from manning the tour guide microphone for the paddle-steamer to running the tea and coffee saloon.

As we pulled up at the winery, he smiled at me. 'I've got it now. I've been trying to work out who you are and I've got it.'

I smiled back at him.

'You're Jeff Kennett's brother, aren't you!'

I sort of nodded; it would have been impolite to do anything else and I wondered if the former Victorian premier even had a brother, let alone if I resembled him in any discernible way. I ended up buying a lot of wine, but whether that was because of the crew member's comments I can't remember.

I also managed to spill some of the wine I tasted onto my shirt, to go with the orange.

So near the end of my hit and run holiday to Mildura I decided to make use of the much heralded laundry at the beautiful old Grand Hotel to do more than a 'traveller's wash' – which, in my aunty Rita's opinion, was international parlance for washing 'the smalls' in the shower and then hanging them over the rail to dry.

I used the coins in my pocket for the wash cycle but needed some change from the bar for the dryer. I checked the dryer and saw that, although the cycle had stopped, there were clothes in it.

They looked dry.

What should I do? Wait for the owners to collect their clothes?

I thought I could buy myself some time by getting the change. While I was away perhaps whoever owned the clothes would come and collect them.

Arriving at the bar, I chatted over my dilemma while I sipped on a frothy.

The bar staff, two thirty-somethings, were helpful. Perhaps I should borrow a plastic bag and place the clothes in it? Then put it on top of the dryer?

Thirty-something one said, 'Yeah, that'd be okay.'

I sipped my beer.

Maybe I should fold them too? Just to be polite?

Thirty-something two offered, 'They're not damp, so you're not poaching a dryer mid-dry. That definitely isn't the go.'

I nodded.

'Crap,' said thirty-something one. 'I was backpacking in India and I hadn't washed for a week. I got to this place where there's a washing machine and a shower. A supreme pizza!'

Thirty-something two laughed, nodding her head. 'I know what you mean. You come across a place like that, you make the most of it.'

'Yeah, of course you do. So I whack the washing on the long cycle and go have a proper shower – one that works, with hot water!'

'This place sounds like it's too good to be true.'

Thirty-something one held up his hand. 'Wait, there's more.'

I resisted a smile.

'I come out of the shower, take the washing out of the machine and put it in the dryer.'

'They had a dryer?' Thirty-something two was incredulous.

Thirty-something one nodded.

'This isn't going to end well, is it?' Thirty-something two smiled.

'I think, it's a beautiful night, I'll just pop down on the floor and have a quick TME.'

'What's a TME?' I asked.

'Tantric meditation exercise.'

'Oh,' I said.

'Yeah, just a quick one where you inhale and then slowly release your breaths to counts of two and keep going while you drift off into relaxation and connect with your thoughts.'

'And what happened?' asked thirty-something two.

'While I'm relaxing and feeling really connected to everything, some shit comes in and dumps my half-dry clothes on top of the dryer. Just leaves them there.'

'Didn't you hear them? I mean, you were relaxing on the floor weren't you?' I asked.

Thirty-something one shrugged his shoulders. 'Must have gone deeper than I thought. I sort of felt a bit disturbed but I breathed through it, everything was going so sweetly for me – finding the bathroom, the shower and laundry.'

He paused.

'That's a bummer,' said thirty-something two.

'Yeah, I think it was this French couple.' He breathed out then he looked straight at me. 'Thought somebody else would do your washing.' He sounded appalled and a little disappointed.

'Why?'

'Well, you're Sam Newman.'

Who should be more upset – Sam Newman from the AFL *Footy Show* or me? He's spent a lot more time and money looking the way he does. As for me, I was too stunned to take much offence. And I suspect that Sam is a lot fitter than me. So. Call it a draw.

But wait, there's more.

I went off with a plastic bag to the dryer.

I stood folding clothes. Some are politely called 'smalls'. Undies. I was folding strangers' undies. And these were undies no stranger should touch, let alone fold. They were interesting. Leave it at that.

Just as I considered stuffing them in the plastic bag, there was a voice.

'What are you doing?'

I turned and stared at a pleasant, generous-looking woman.

I went to say something before I thought what it was I wanted to say. So I stopped and tried to think, which meant I stood like a sack of spuds with my mouth open.

'Why are you holding my husband's underpants?'

'Is that what you call them?' I tried to not look guilty while I explained, but the woman stopped me.

'Do I know you?'

I tossed up between admitting I was the Demtel man or Sam Newman. Or Jeff Kennett's brother. Maybe even Colin Firth. Or Mark Latham. Yes, I would own to being any of them as I stood holding a strange man's 'underpants'.

The term underpants somehow didn't do the right thing by the garments I clutched. Underpants were way too modest and functional a description of these . . . bits of animal-print string.

Somehow the thought of Mark Latham holding these things was a bit too much to bear, so I decided to try to explain.

I closed my mouth. Then opened it. Maybe Mark Latham wasn't so bad a thing to be.

'You're William McInnes,' the woman said, 'off the telly! I've read your books.'

We laughed. Me uncomfortably.

Next morning, when I was checking out, my friend from the laundry came up to me. With her husband. He was just as generous as she.

'You've had your hands in my undies,' said the man.

'And mine!' said my laundry friend.

As it happens, Col the coach driver was waiting nearby for his day's tourist passengers. He winked. 'You lucky bugger!'

Well, something to chat about at Orange World.

•

The great thing about hit and run holidays is that because they are so compacted, you try to make the most of the time you have. The result of this is that you become a bit more inclined to roll with whatever the hit and run holiday throws up at you. If there is a hiccup that leaves you waiting, you try to make the most of the time.

The bloke behind the desk at the air terminal had a porn-star mo and aviator sunnies. He shook his head.

'No flying for a while, matey. Too much smoke from the bushfires. Cool your heels for a few hours and we'll see how we go in the afternoon.'

Four hours of my life to give up to Hobart.

As a kid, Hobart had a certain aura about it. The place the big yacht race ended and where all the winners from TV quiz shows would be sent as a reward for their brilliance. 'To stay at the Wrest Point Casino!' the voiceover man boomed.

Those were the days. Only casino in Australia. It had even impressed Trevor Tait of Trevor Tait Travel enough to be the one holiday he had actually taken.

I had stayed at the casino hotel on a previous visit to Tasmania.

I had gone down to have drink at the bar on a Friday night and sat, stunned, as I realised I was the oldest person having a gargle by nearly three decades.

I thought the clientele must have been wearing school uniforms a few hours earlier in the day and then taken them off for a night at Wrest Point, they were all so young.

I asked the barman, who reminded me of the character Lloyd the barman from the film *The Shining*, whether there was a formal on that night.

He looked back at me and said, 'Sorry, mate?'

'A formal, a school formal.'

We looked at each other and then around the room, and I had to admit that the clothes being worn weren't the sorts you actually see at a school formal.

'No, mate, just the usual Friday night crowd.'

I nodded, finished my drink and went back upstairs to my room and watched the telly.

The next night was like some *Back to the Future* rebooting. Lloyd the barman was there in his same outfit and the place was as full as it had been the night before. Only I was the youngest by about three decades and maybe more.

It was as if everybody had moved to the opposite end of the adult life cycle, like a sped-up nature film or some mad plot device from a science fiction film.

I looked at Lloyd. 'You'd go silly if you tried to count the cardigans here tonight,' I said.

Lloyd looked back at me. 'Sorry, mate?'

'This lot.' I waved at the Cardigans, which seemed a pretty good word to describe a collective of older-aged casino-goers.

Lloyd looked around. 'Just the usual Saturday night crowd, mate.'

I nodded, finished my drink and went back upstairs to my room to watch the telly.

The hotel's gym was even more fascinating. It looked like another design by the professor from *Gilligan's Island*, who, as well as creating the Perth pedal cars, was a pretty interesting character. He was a high school science teacher and well-known scoutmaster, which sounds like a police bulletin, but we'll leave it there.

The gym was some of his best work; all that was missing were the obligatory coconut dumbbells and ropes made from vines but everything else seemed as though it had been made out of found objects.

The place was empty, save for a vast man in a tight, bright orange and black striped jumpsuit. He stood staring at himself in a mirror. He stood there for a good while.

As Lloyd the barman would have said, 'Just your average early morning crowd.'

I went back upstairs to my room and watched telly.

But this hit and run holiday was different – I only had four hours to kill before I had to fly.

Hobart.

What to do for four hours?

I looked at the bloke behind the airport desk.

'Mate, do they still have tours to the Cadbury factory?'

He stared back and I saw myself reflected in his sunglasses.

He didn't seem to think that much of the idea.

In my defence, I had a deep-seated fondness for those school excursions to the Golden Circle Cannery, the Big Pineapple and the Nambour Sugar Mill.

Hobart is a beautiful city, perhaps the prettiest of Australian capitals, with marvellous restaurants and glorious landscapes. There had to be something I could do. The bloke behind the desk brushed one side of his porn star's moustache with his forefinger and then said, 'Go to the museum, mate. Museum's a good place.'

The museum. It could only mean one place: the Museum of Old and New Art (MONA), an entirely privately funded institution that has captured the imagination of Tasmanians and visitors alike.

•

There were crowds outside the museum. I found myself listening to the conversations going on around me.

'Should we have brought the kids here?' asked a father. 'Maybe they would have liked to go to the chocolate factory.'

'Oh, Brian, we've been through this!' said his wife. 'Coral reckoned the choccy factory's a real letdown. A pretty tame video and they let you loose in the shop.'

MONA certainly wasn't tame and the number of kids wandering through the floors was pleasant but also a tad startling. Some of the art collection is a bit extreme and challenging. Why you'd chance young kids peering at such work is anybody's guess, but as long as it's better value than Cadbury's, that's okay.

The eclectic scale and verve of the collection is stupefying, moving and glorious.

There's the poo machine. An installation by the Belgian artist Wim Delvoye that is basically anti-art. Or supremely silly fun. A series of tubes and pipes and amphora-shaped glass vessels replicate the human digestive tract. Food is placed in each chamber and enzymes are added by a neat-bearded, happy attendant. Digestion begins.

After four hours people marvel at farting sounds as a Mister Whippy swirl of artistic faeces emerges on a plate.

It pulls quite a crowd. A well-known federal cabinet minister and her family all sat down on the floor with the rest of us MONA punters to enjoy the show. A man behind me had recognised the cabinet minister and whispered to somebody he was with, 'I suppose she's just used to being a politician. Waiting for a shit to drop must feel like a pretty good day in parliament.'

After poo, where else would you go than the death gallery? A huge queue, including me, waited to be allowed entry.

I heard a fed-up old bloke behind me say to his daughter, 'Oh, do we really have to go to the death gallery? This sex and death is all very well but I am absolutely starving.'

They laughed and headed off. I took their cue: it was time to fly.

Sex, death, queues and four fabulous hours in beautiful Hobart. The bloke with the porn star moustache was right, that 'Museum's a good place.'

•

Not everyone is fond of golf and that's a shame because it is a game that wraps itself around a hit and run holiday perfectly.

It pays, though, to have an honest perspective on your own ability. There is really no reason to think you are anything but a hack out for a nice stroll and a chat with a mate, and in between you hit a little white ball in every direction except the one it's supposed to head.

My friend Rob and I had just managed to finish a round of 1970s golf. We call the style of game we play after that particular decade because our scores are so inflationary, just like the inflation rates of the good old days of the oil crisis. When we're really on song we allow ourselves to creep into the 1980s and particular holes are called Malcolm Frasers because both of us achieve double-digit scores, just like old Mal's 1982 effort of recording double-digit unemployment and inflation.

After the game Rob said he would buy lunch.

Since it's holiday time we can treat ourselves. For middle-aged men who have known each other for years that means junk food.

Just how long we have been playing seventies golf on hit and run holidays I'm not sure, but I've known Rob since uni. Over that time neither our golf nor our meal choices have changed.

So it's junk food for lunch.

'Hamburgers,' he said.

'I haven't had a hamburger for yonks,' I said excitedly. 'We used to get hamburgers a lot after a round.'

Rob said he had one the other day and it was 'All right'.

In boofhead food parlance, 'all right' is as high a piece of praise as can be uttered.

Rob said we'd get drive-through. Alarm bells began in my brain.

Call me a snob, but any food ordered through a microphone while seated in a vehicle can never be given the 'all right' rating.

'When you say this hamburger was all right,' I asked, 'did you mean all right or okay?'

We laughed but there was a difference.

'Okay,' he said.

'All right' rates way higher than 'okay' and Rob knew it.

I didn't want a hamburger from Macca's or Hungry Jack's. Both are fine if you are in a particular mood, I am sure, but not after a 1970s golf round.

'No, come on,' Rob said, 'we'll get them from KFC.'

He sounded twelve.

'KFC?' I sounded like Lady Bracknell talking about handbags.

I'm old enough to remember that KFC was Kentucky Fried Chicken until it was rebranded and the advertisers got Elle Macpherson to try to spruik the fried food.

''Cause I like it like that,' said Ms Macpherson in a breathy voice and then she proceeded to take an incredibly unenthusiastic nibble at a bit of the colonel's finest fried bird, as if it was a dried dog turd being offered to her.

Presumably old Kentucky Fried was turned into initials because it sounded healthier, and getting a late twentieth-century supermodel to sell it glammed up the eleven secret herbs and spices.

'Kentucky Fried Chicken doesn't do hamburgers.'

'What?' Rob asked.

It's like this. A hamburger is a hamburger. It comes from fish and chip shops or milk bars. Or school tuckshops, fetes or shows.

It's holiday food. It's a bit rough-hewn and knockabout. No perfectly rounded white sugary buns in cardboard boxes. No anonymous frozen 'patties'.

It's a hamburger. A thing of terror or beauty. An epic fight in a bun, with beetroot, pineapple, cheese and shredded carrot spilling about.

A beef rissole shaped like Uluru wrapped in a cloak of bacon.

They earn names, these hamburgers. Not from marketing divisions in airless, air-conditioned rooms, but from the people who eat the things.

Like the Blodwyn Burger from a fish and chip shop in Scarborough, named because the burger was the size of my mother's Jack Russell terrier Blodwyn and also because that burger made you fart like the dog.

The Big Artie was from a roadhouse outside of Rocky after a round of seventies golf in Yeppoon in conditions that were close to cyclonic. But the Big Artie made up for it all; it was so big it took almost as long to eat as playing the round of golf.

'Why'd you call it the Big Artie?' I asked.

The bloke who had cooked it just stared at me as if I were an idiot.

'Just like Artie Beetson, mate,' he said.

Artie Beetson was the giant rugby league legend who was a household name throughout the Sunshine state.

'It's big, it's made here in Queensland and it never lets you down. Why wouldn't you call it Big Artie?'

The Battle of Culloden was a hamburger made by an angry Scottish bloke in a Fremantle takeaway. It was like trying to eat something alive and he put so much sauce and beetroot on it that, after eating it, your face looked like it had been clubbed to pieces.

And no mass-produced, drive-through product could ever be used to describe a great love, as Rob once had, saying the woman he loved was 'a hamburger with the lot'.

So no, no drive-through burger for me.

This was where the hit and run holiday started to go a bit south.

Rob pulled out a flyer that had been placed on the windscreen of his car while we were hacking our way through eighteen holes of time-travelling golf.

The flyer proclaimed a 'Sportsman's' Special'.

'This was meant to be,' said Rob. 'It's a two-for-one deal.'

'And we are sportsmen,' I added.

'We so definitely are.'

The steak looked good on the poster: char-grill marks, seasoning. And the hotel was cool, gracious and comfortable. It didn't seem like a place that would try to pass off an ordinary piece of beef.

This impromptu choice for a seventies golf lunch looked okay.

'Two for one?' said Rob and he thought for moment before admitting that the phrase described our golfing ability. 'Why take one shot to get the ball where it's supposed to be going when you can take two, or three or five?'

'Or six or seven,' I added.

'Two for one?' he said again, this time to the woman behind the bar.

'Two for one,' the pleasant woman assured us, adding, 'and all you can eat from the salad and vegetable bar, plus you get a serve of chips.'

'Two for one!' Rob said this a little too eagerly. We got two beers and sat down.

The beers were good. The day was hot. And Sydney, even here on the leafy north side of the bridge, was cramped; bristling and swollen.

Perhaps that's why it always feels like there are so many people in Sydney. The footpaths are crowded with a mass of accents, phone conversations and impatience. Everybody seems to want to be somewhere else. I'd come to the city for a holiday and so I was really noticing people's attitude.

When you're on holidays you mostly go at your own pace, dawdling in and around a city's citizens as they go about their business.

Except the man on George Street that morning who'd shoved a pamphlet at me like an army cook doling out rations when I was waiting to be picked up by Rob.

'Make the most of the time you've got left. Make sure you make your peace.' It was a pamphlet about the predicted end of the world according to the Mayan calendar. Apparently it was going to happen at dawn on the 21st of December. Do differing time zones come into play when the world ends? I had a sad feeling we'd been through all this before.

Sydney is so beautiful from so many vantage points. So many postcard moments. The bridge, the harbour, the Opera House, the eastern beaches, the gardens, the ferries, on and on and on.

So many people taking photos.

Like the Chinese sailors in the corner of the two-for-one steak hotel. They were on shore leave and it seemed a common pastime for visiting sailors was photo taking.

The group in the corner stood in front of a poker machine called Cooee Country; it was an outback-themed game with cockatoos, kangaroos and suitably camp 'Australian' looking characters. I wondered if Baz Luhrmann had started to design pokies.

Waiting for the radio buzzer to inform us our 'two for one' steaks were ready, Rob and I sipped our beers and watched a replay of an old cricket one-dayer. I knew it was old because Carl Rackemann was a thrilling young prospect. A young sailor stood staring up at the screen and then laughed, shrugged his shoulders and sat back down with his shipmates.

Carl was pretty good.

I suddenly thought of the old *Redcliffe Herald* and how it would pop photos in of service personnel on overseas duty, as if that was the only reason why anybody would want to leave the peninsula. I thought of the bloke named Len Fox from Woody Point crouching in the jungles of Vietnam. I looked at the sailors and wondered how Len had made out after his 'holiday'; how he might be now.

The buzzer went off and the steak looked great. We made the most of the all-you-can-eat salad bar and vegies.

We ate. The steak was like Hubba Bubba. So chewy you could almost blow bubbles.

'I knew it was too good to be true,' said Rob.

We both laughed like drains.

I felt something rustle in my pocket. The end of the world according to the Mayans.

'Too good to be true,' I said, and took great delight in tearing the pamphlet up and sprinkling it on the inedible steak.

In the corner Cooee Country went off and the Chinese sailors yelled in delight, quickly taking another photo of themselves.

•

The more things change, sometimes it seems the more they stay the same. It was holidays, school holidays tacked onto Easter. We hadn't been away and I think that was why my daughter decided it would be fun to organise a hit and run holiday in the Middle Ages. It seemed a nice mixture, hitting and running and the Middle Ages, and an appropriate choice since I was middle-aged.

It turned out to be a wonderful hit and run holiday to a Ma and Pa Kettle dinosaur that somehow seemed to have survived the corporatisation of the holiday experience.

Kryal Castle it was called, and it was the brainchild of a fellow called Keith Ryal, who had a great vision of a Ma and Pa Kettle tourist park and built a medieval castle at the base of Mount Warrenheip, just outside Ballarat.

It looked convincing enough in a Tony Curtis *Black Shield of Falworth*, 1950s sword-and-armour matinee kind of way but what makes it wonderful is the sense of incongruity.

The most striking thing about Kryal Castle is the great telecommunications tower that looms over it. Second is the fact that anybody thought about building a medieval castle in the first place.

True, Ballarat does have Sovereign Hill, which is a holiday park based around the Australian minefields with lots of people role-playing troopers and miners during the gold rush. But it's connected to Australian colonial history in the local area.

The castle is so crazily not connected to our past that it's a wonder it's still there. Okay, so a few people in England, or wherever, lived in a few castles and this continent was colonised by the English.

It is a long bow to draw. And that's why it's so much fun.

Kryal Castle is like somebody's hobby gone toxic, as if nobody ever said: 'Now come on, that's enough, stop it.' And that's what was so much fun about this serious dose of 'Kevin Costneritis'. Appropriately, it was while we were watching *Field of Dreams* that my daughter had the idea of doing a hit and run to Kryal Castle.

One of the joys of multiple free-to-air TV channels is the way certain movies are endlessly repeated. Like *Love, Actually*, any of the *Lethal Weapon* or *Terminator* franchises or *Pretty Woman*. It's like being caught in a bad hotel room where the in-room entertainment options stop at 1999.

It's a chance to share some of your youthful pop culture with your children. Not long ago on the box up popped another rerun favourite: *Field of Dreams* with Kevin Costner.

Kevin's a farmer who bulldozes his wheat crop and builds a baseball field. Ghosts of famous baseball players emerge from the crop and begin playing.

Kevin made the field because he heard a voices whispering to him, 'Build it and they will come.'

'Hey, it's that baseball picture!' my son yelled out.

'Yeah,' I cried.

'Which one?' yelled my daughter.

We like baseball movies in our house.

'Is it the one with angels in the outfield?' asked my daughter.

'It's *Field of Dreams*,' I told her.

'Yeah,' said my son. 'The one with the creepy voice whispering to that old guy.'

My son was talking about Kevin Costner, in all his late-eighties, early-nineties glory.

I asked my daughter what she thought of young Kev in his white shirt, tight jeans, and his hair – a little too highlighted – swept back over his head in a modest fountain mullet.

She considered it for a while. 'He looks like he wants to burp.'

He did look like he wanted to let one rip. A bit liverish and full to the brim after eating too much.

Sadly, Kev was trying to look sexy in his late-eighties, early-nineties way. My daughter had a point; just thinking of that time made me want to belch too.

And then we heard the whispering voice. 'Build it and they will come.'

'And that's why he builds a baseball thing in his crop?' my daughter asked incredulously.

I nodded.

'Dad, don't ever say anything I watch is garbage – ever.'

I looked at Kev and felt like a Quick-eze.

'If you build it – they will come' – a stupid phrase and one many people may have heard to their regret.

We are all Kevin Costner at times. Take the bunch that thought up the almost mythic concept of a Space City at Kallangur. It was a clutch of odd concrete buildings constructed with inflatable plastic dome moulds. Never really worked. My aunt lamented, 'They aimed for space and came up short in Kallangur. Never mind, the butcher always had lovely veal.'

When you've had an attack of Kevin Costneritis and reached for the sky, you can end up landing pretty hard in Kallangur.

Or you can also find yourself with Kryal Castle, which may be somewhere between the two.

We wisely decided to extend our stay in the Middle Ages by booking in for a 'medieval experience' with modern-day four-star luxuries. That meant a room with no windows, tapestries everywhere, beds with ornate, carved bed heads and a mini bar, television and room-service menu.

The room-service menu let us know we could enjoy a hearty feast of medieval delights, such as fried flat-tails and chips or special fried rice.

The television, much to my son's disappointment, was only free to air. 'Stuff the Middle Ages, there's no Foxtel!' he said, flipping through the channels.

Inside the castle was where the action really took place. Before we arrived, we read that we would be welcomed by people in 'Middle Ages garb'. My daughter asked if that meant everybody would be adorned with glasses and wearing chinos, Rodd & Gunn shirts, and loafers. 'You know, like you, Dad!'

There were some people dressed like that but she needn't have worried because they were other patrons, and we were greeted at the front desk by a medieval maid of honour with the thickest Indian accent I had heard in some time. Which, I suppose, is a pretty good reflection of multi-racial modern Australia.

The maid helpfully told us where to start the adventure. 'Just down that hallway and to the right – not left because you'll end up in the back of the death and torture gallery. Have a lovely stay!'

Inside the castle grounds there was some jousting. We sat in a grandstand with a fair crowd of people and looked down on people in armour beating each other up. People ate hot dogs, sandwiches and chips while some hokey story about honour and chivalry was played out.

The master of ceremonies invited us 'honoured lords and ladies' to partake of the castle's vast array of refreshments – potato cakes, Chiko rolls and other snacks were available for purchase.

It all seemed a bit half-arsed but in an entertaining enough way. People put themselves in stocks, Australia's own torture racks, and then smiled for the camera.

I chatted to a man dressed as a herald, who also happened to be a manager at the castle.

I asked him how the Middle Ages were treating him.

'Oh, been a bit tough,' he said. He wasn't talking about the plague, regicide or religious wars and intrigue but something more insidious.

Bad weather.

'Been a little quiet, this holidays, although this week has been all right.'

He waved at a 'knight' in chest armour, board shorts and runners, who was cleaning up some paraphernalia from that day's battle.

'It's a pretty big place,' I said, looking around the castle.

He nodded. 'Yeah, a lot of upkeep costs.'

Well, why wouldn't there be? It was a castle, after all; I can imagine King Arthur having the same sort of worries at Camelot.

'There's been all sorts of ideas with what to do with this place,' said the herald-cum-manager. 'Somebody floated the idea of turning it into a brothel but,' he smiled, 'that was never going to happen. Not out here.'

Later on when the park was closed we had the run of the castle and went back to the arena to play with all the gear left in the huts. We ran around in the dusk light, belting each other with foam swords, maces and balls on chains that bounced off like soft balloons. A magpie sang goodbye to another hit and run holiday and to the Middle Ages, Ballarat-style.

Driving back to Melbourne along the highway you can see a ghost of hit and run holidays from the past. It's in Rockbank, and although it's fading fast, you can still see a hint of what once existed. In amongst prefabricated cement factories and showrooms, there's a strange Besser-block building, almost like a pillbox, the last remnants of a sprawling complex.

I remembered that almost every state had one.

You can see it best when the sun begins to set and it almost glows. Braiding the top of the lonely little cement box are the faded remains of yellow and black safari markings. And below, in large lettering, blazes out the ghostly promise of adventure and hit and run holiday magic – 'LIONS SAFARI'.

Wind up your windows.

Pet-friendly Holidays

It was Ray and Delilah's first holiday and both were silly as wheels and lovely beyond all description.

Even though they looked like rather helpless, greeting-card puppies, they were in fact a pair of pleasant nut jobs.

On the first morning of our stay at the beach we wandered out onto the deck for cups of tea and coffee.

Leon, a mate who had come with us, noticed the holes in the yard. And the droppings. And the general mess caused by the two puppies. We stood surveying the backyard, or what was left of it.

'Jeez, Will, you should call them Rio and Tinto instead of Ray and Delilah.'

'Why's that?'

'Because all they do is dig big holes and leave a lot of shit behind.'

Ray and Delilah had been a Christmas present to us and are very friendly dogs. Overwhelmingly friendly.

The thought that any corporate entity could be as friendly as them is quite frankly disturbing. On occasion, when for example you give them a pat after being away from them for a day, they urinate with excitement.

Later that day an elderly lady who lived around the corner and who walked along the beach every morning and night said hello to the dogs as I struggled with them on a leash on the steps to the beach.

She was lovely, but rather deaf.

'Hello there, sweethearts,' she cooed.

Ray and then Delilah bounded up and down on the spot, wagging tails like high-speed propellers, and let rip with a gush of pee that would have done any fire hydrant proud.

'Oh now, there you are, you're as bad as my Arnie,' the lady said as Ray kept ripping.

I said sorry on behalf of the hounds but the old lady wasn't fazed.

'He's definitely got a touch of Arnold about him,' she said patting Ray. 'Arnold's my husband. Goes off like a rocket.'

'Oh yes?' I said. I didn't really want to think about what Ray and Arnie had in common.

'What are their names?'

'Raymond and Delilah,' I said as clearly as I could.

'Oh right, from the Bible stories. Lovely.'

I had to think for a bit. Then I understood.

Samson and Delilah. Raymond and Delilah. Fair enough, but it still made me laugh.

'Lovely names,' said the old lady.

I wondered if there was a Ray in the Bible. I bet you he'd have been a friendly disciple.

Just as long as he didn't pee when he got excited.

•

'You know, I don't think I have ever met a nasty Ray,' my friend Niall said the next day, 'or one who has urinated so much.'

Ray and Delilah were excited to see Niall and me because that morning we had decided it would be a good idea to go to Gunnamatta for, of all things, a horse ride. The fact that only one of our party of nine could ride properly didn't really come into the equation. It was a holiday – and the flyer at the general store claimed that the riding school covered all levels of experience.

And all ranges of weight up to 100 kilos, which was a good thing.

There was no point in lying about your weight as the more suspicious-looking members of our posse were forced to stand on industrial-looking scales and their weight was shrieked out by one of the riding employees.

We were given hairnets for hygiene and helmets and told to mount our steeds.

Mine was a heavy-duty Clydesdale called Audrey and Niall's was a friendly looking hobbler by the name of Minnie.

We heaved ourselves up and walked around the yards in a circle formation.

The shrieking weight revealer gave us some valuable advice, 'Don't kick the horse with your heels until you are told and remember, when it comes to this trip, the horse is smarter than you.'

And we were off. At a walk first and then a canter. That was as fast as it got but it was obvious that the horses knew the trail like the back of their hoof so there was no point in trying to do anything to control them.

'It's like it's on autopilot,' said a friend of my son.

'More like auto-rider!' corrected the shrieking weight revealer.

It was when we were going down the trail beside the road that things got a little strained.

The noise that was starting to come from certain members of our posse was indecent if you closed your eyes.

Groans. Emissions of noise that you might expect to hear from a bad porno soundtrack mixed with a gladiator film.

All courtesy of Minnie and Niall.

His hygienic hairnet had fallen down below his helmet and had covered his sunglasses. When he tried to correct what was going on he dropped the reins.

'I've dropped the ropes,' he yelled.

'You mean reins,' somebody said.

'Oh Christ, whatever they are, I've dropped them.'

'Grab the saddle pommel,' said the shrieking weight revealer rather calmly. 'Minnie will know what to do.'

Niall did as he was told, but needed two hands to make him stable.

'I can't see, I can't see!' he yelled.

In between his yelling, he began laughing. Some might call it odd but it was impossible not to laugh along with it.

Minnie's rather interesting method of movement resembled a cross between an agitated exercise bike and a jackhammer, and it elicited even more grunts, groans, oaths and vibrato warbles of discomfort from Niall.

It sounded as if he was doing an impersonation of the old, trembling-voiced French crooner Charles Aznavour trying to perform with his vitals caught in his zipper.

The other horses started to follow suit. Actually, the horses were lovely creatures who knew exactly what they were doing. The problem was us.

We had no idea.

And we were starting to sound like an incredibly out-of-tune a cappella group who were all using completely different song sheets.

Amidst all this rather undignified noise came Niall shrieking, 'Bugger me, I'm like Helen Keller riding in the bloody Melbourne Cup. I can't see a thing!'

Somehow, eventually, we all reached the beach and were lined up for a photo.

The surf crashed behind us and a few of the horses turned their heads slightly at the noise.

'This isn't far from where Harold Holt disappeared, you know,' said Leon.

'Well, if it was a choice between taking the Chinese submarine or riding back on Minnie's great-grandmother then no wonder he went under,' muttered Niall, trying to straighten his hairnet.

•

The other thing we had treated ourselves to that Christmas holiday was a large digital projector, which we set up on the deck outside.

As well, we borrowed an old radiogram with that wonderful cloth weave with streaks of gold thread shining through and a big booming speaker system that sounded like an old cinema.

We'd kick back and enjoy widescreen movies on the side of the house; holding our eclectic film festival.

For some reason we decided on a series of double bills, starting with episodes of the old Australian television classic *Skippy the Bush Kangaroo*, which was bizarrely entertaining.

We followed it up with films such as *Trainspotting*, the comedy drama about drug addiction and poverty in Edinburgh in the late nineties; *On the Beach*, the apocalyptic tale of the end of the world where the last city alive is Melbourne; *The Last of the Knucklemen*, an old 1970s Australian classic about a mining gang in the outback; and *Jaws* 1, 2 and 3D!

Skippy would draw some of the local kids out to watch the adventures of the bush kangaroo.

The problematic moment came when *Skippy* finished and then Ewan McGregor disappeared down a toilet in

Trainspotting, and we heard little voices screeching in shock and muttered comments from parents: 'No, no, it's all right, it's not Skippy, it's just another film.'

And the little ones were led away.

Skippy was a favourite, though. There was something about the show that everyone could tap into. The oddity, the memories for those who had watched it as a child.

The colour was like those family photographs in old albums, rich and slightly sepia toned.

The storylines were, of course, incredible, with Skippy the bush kangaroo driving a boat, playing drums in a 'rock' group and dialling a phone. My daughter and her friends didn't know what was more interesting: that a kangaroo could dial a phone or that phones used to have something as quaintly appealing as a dial.

And then there were the appallingly wonderful performances. Tony Bonner and Ed Devereaux were the best.

Tony Bonner was the park helicopter pilot who never left the ground. Every episode would end with a shot of the helicopter sitting on its pad out the back of the rangers' headquarters, with its propellers slowly turning.

I can remember how my father would laugh at Tony Bonner's efforts to look like he knew what he was doing as he poked and pointed to bits and pieces of the aircraft.

'This poor bastard has no idea of what he's doing, look! Look at him!' my father would yell and we would all watch as the handsome, violently blond actor pranced unconvincingly about the helicopter.

We thought it hilarious.

He specialised in 'stationary flying acting', where he wobbled and jumped around in a seat, peered about and spoke loudly into his microphone.

'Ed Dev', as Mr Devereaux became known during our film festival, was the park ranger and widower, who along with his two sons and Jerry, Bonner's seated flyer, had adventures with Skippy. There was also 'Clancy' Merrick, the only woman in the show, who stays with the Hammonds.

Ed Dev had the tones of his generation: that crazy Anglified accent where each syllable and consonant was hit and enunciated. He also wore the most unflattering pair of khaki ranger pants that have seen the light of day. They were pressed to within an inch of their lives, with the effect that, while every other part of his trousers were sharp and clean, his crotch area looked like an accordion being played by a drunk in some bad Irish-themed pub.

He stood up and sat down so much we started to make accordion sounds when he went about his business.

We had a 'talk like Ed Dev day', which everyone joined in with gusto and, even more annoyingly for the other patrons of the general store, we ate breakfast like Tony Bonner, shifting about in our chairs and wobbling our heads.

'Walk like Tony' was an exercise where you walked about on the balls of your feet, as Tony Bonner seemed to do in his desert-boots chasing bushrangers that turned into a 'rock group' practising in a cave in the park.

It was hard to believe that it was Australia we were seeing represented and how much it had changed since I was a kid.

Although if people are enjoying something I have appeared in forty or so years after it is made then I will count myself very fortunate.

As for Indigenous Australia, the bush kangaroo was patronisingly well meaning. Indigenous actors were either kept to playing exotic savages or, in the case of one actor who looked simply amazing, his voice was dubbed by someone who sounded like James Dibble, the veteran ABC newsreader.

'How did they train the kangaroo to do the stuff with its paws?' one of the kids asked.

Niall broke the truth delightedly. 'It wasn't the kangaroo; it was somebody using two kangaroo-paw bottle openers. I couldn't believe it when my brothers told me but it's true: bottle openers.'

There was a bit of a silence and then disbelief until Niall demonstrated what could be done with two old-fashioned bottle openers. He hid down in front of the widescreen image and then put his extended 'Skippy' paws over the ones on the side of the house.

'That is sort of awful but kind of cool,' said one young audience member.

A koala growled in a treetop around the side of the house and when Ed Dev was talking about being a widower I stared and remembered how all these animal shows of the sixties had a parent missing.

Lassie had a family without a father, while *Flipper*, about an adventurous dolphin, followed the *Skippy* template with a widowed father and two sons.

I pointed this out in a distant sort of voice and then nobody said anything much as Ed Dev accordioned his way across the gravel drive while Tony Bonner Tony-walked beside him, making their way to a beautiful old Falcon station wagon.

Then my daughter said, 'Dad, can we get another animal?'

There was a silence. On the screen Ed Dev looked shocked and we all burst out laughing.

A koala growled around the side of the house.

'How about we have that koala?' said my son.

'Koalas just growl and get stoned on gum leaves,' said Niall.

The koala growled again and Niall said, 'Shut up and go back to bed, Stoner.'

Ray and Delilah began to bark, whether it was at the koala or Ed Dev's accordions we couldn't tell.

'What would the Hammonds do with Skippy when they went on holiday?' Niall asked after a moment.

Delilah had crept around the front of the projector and was staring at the beams of light with a manic intensity that only a Kelpie can possess.

'They'd leave her there,' someone said.

'But would they? I mean you've taken Ray and Delilah – why wouldn't they take Skippy?'

'You can't take a kangaroo with you on holidays,' said one of the kids.

Niall got up to get a beer. 'Well, you can take the important bits of him, the paws with the bottle opener.'

Delilah began leaping up at the beams of light and snapping her jaws with a lapping sound. Stoner growled some more. Ed Dev looked cranky and raised an eyebrow.

Niall shook his head as he limped back.

'Fond memories of Minnie the horse, Niall?'

'Bloody Minnie. It's been a while since my vitals have felt like this – if she was a woman I'd marry her. Though, I have to say, as a rule of thumb, most animals and holidays don't mix.'

'Oh come on,' I said. 'You were the one who dropped the "ropes".'

'Bugger Minnie!' he said. 'If she was a donkey I would have eaten her. I did that one holiday.'

Tony Bonner looked at his helicopter and said, 'That sounds crazy, Matt.'

'No, it's true.' Niall nodded up to the side of the house at a puzzled-looking Tony and a suspicious Ed Dev.

'You ate donkey?' asked Leon.

'Yeah, donkey sausages with Jesus.'

'I've got to hear this,' said Leon.

Delilah snapped at the light and somebody blew a gum leaf.

It all began when Niall was walking the Camino de Santiago trail, a route of pilgrimage to the supposed resting place of St James in northwestern Spain. Thousands of people set out to walk the trail, some for the religious pilgrimage and others just for the trek.

'The strange thing about the pilgrimage is that so much of it is sealed road,' said Niall. 'You'd think it'd be dusty tracks and little villages but a lot of it is along a major highway.'

'So that's why you ate the donkey?'

'Well, yes, sort of, the sealed road just completely stuffs your feet and mine blistered really badly.'

The roads along the Camino de Santiago can become so hot in the summer that some pilgrims or hikers can be quite incapacitated.

In Niall's case, it was so bad he could walk no further and had to stay at a hostel run by a self-proclaimed healer called Jesus.

'Don't believe it.'

'Google him,' Niall said with a wiggle of his fingers.

'Google Jesus?'

'Not *the* Jesus, this Jesus. He's a bit of a healer.'

'Is he?'

The koala growled.

'Yes he is, Stoner, and he said I could stay at this hostel of his while my feet got better.'

'What did this guy look like?' I asked.

'Like Jesus,' snorted Niall. 'Long hair and beard. He gave me a steel brush.'

'For your blisters?'

'No, for the wall. We were cleaning a wall. He said it would take my mind off my feet.'

'Did it?'

'Well, no, the fact that I was on my feet cleaning the wall didn't help much. But he would come and talk to me really soothingly while I cleaned the wall and then he pissed off back inside.'

'And the donkey?'

'Jesus fed me sausages. I asked him why they tasted odd and he said they were donkey sausages. And, call me old-fashioned, but I thought that it was poor form for a bloke called Jesus to be eating donkey sausages when donkeys carried his mother to the stable and Jesus rode into Jerusalem on a donkey. That's two big moments that *the* Jesus wouldn't have had without a donkey, and this Jesus was eating donkey snags.'

'Yeah, but it was a different Jesus,' said one of my son's friends.

'Listen, if you're going to run a hostel on a religious pilgrimage, and you're going to call yourself Jesus – *Jesus* – then I think you have certain responsibilities to the brand.'

Leon asked what happened to Niall's feet.

'Well, thank Christ —'

'*The* Christ?'

'Yes, *the* Christ. Thank *the* Christ that a couple of girls I knew turned up in a car.'

On the side of the house Tony Bonner smiled, he liked that idea, and then grumpy Ed Dev shushed him up. Grumpy Ed Dev's porky little boy, who was Skippy's best mate, seemed shocked and looked out towards the deck as well.

By now everybody had turned to Niall.

Only Delilah looked interested in what was happening in Waratah National Park.

'What did you do?' asked my son.

'Well, I got in the car and Jesus came out, he was holding some more donkey sausages, and he said, "Niall, what about the wall?"'

'What did you do?'

'I told him to go jump.'

'You said that to Jesus?'

'Not to *the* Jesus, but to that Jesus, yeah, and I've got to say it was sort of satisfying.'

In the night the koala growled and Delilah snapped at the flickering beams again.

•

Being down at the beach, sitting on a deck with Skippy playing away on the side of the house and with the words of Niall's donkey-sausage dining with Jesus still in the air, I thought about another animal holiday.

'What's up, Timber, got an animal on your mind?' asked Niall.

I nodded. And thought, why not start the story the way it should start, the way you tell a story around a camp fire to school kids. 'It was on a night like this . . .'

There were groans all round.

'Well,' I said, 'it *was* on a night like this. Summer, near the beach, I was on holiday.'

'Who with?' asked my daughter.

'With Doug, Helen and Karl Speck and a blind chicken.'

Where do you start? Helen Speck was gorgeous and I am sure, in time, she could have loved me as much as I loved her. Perhaps love is too refined an emotional concept to describe the way I felt about her. To put it as a friend of mine liked to describe the whole process of sex, I wanted to 'play cross-gender romantic rugby with her'.

She was fully aware how attractive she was and would often walk around the front garden of her home in a series of swimsuits, for no reason that I could understand.

This would drive her father, Doug, around the bend. Douglas Speck loved to shout and seemed perpetually furious. His favourite curse was 'For Christ's sake!' and he would emphasise either 'sake' or 'Christ' depending on how the mood would take him.

'For Christ's *sake* put some decent clothes on, Helen. Parading about in nothing.'

The Specks' front yard was very tidy, with a vast collection of decorative garden gnomes, almost like a tiny army, and Helen would saunter amongst these approving little men.

I never knew how grotesque garden gnomes were until I saw them leering at Helen's attractively alarming late-seventies bikini.

She worked in a Big Rooster on the front counter and would relay the orders through the microphone in her breathy, willowy voice.

She had a way of making everything drip sex. Quarter chicken and chips, pause, pause and then an almost whispered 'with graaaaaavy' would have all us boys in the kitchen almost exploding.

'I love when she says "paradise pack",' said Troy Lipson, who worked the deep-frying troughs with me.

The Big Rooster was owned by her father and on the wall under the words 'Our Friendly Manager' was a photograph of a furiously glowering Douglas Speck.

I saw quite a bit of Helen Speck but not as much as I would have liked to. I had a chance of remedying that when her brother Karl began playing cricket.

He was a big kid, big as a Clydesdale as my father might say, and he was incredibly strong. He never really said much but he always seemed like a good sort of bloke so I cultivated what I thought might be a useful mateship.

I'd go around to the Speck household on the pretence of hanging out with my cricket mate and instead catch an eyeful of Helen wandering about in a pair of her assorted swimmers.

Mrs Speck was a pleasant woman who just smiled benignly as Helen prowled around the gnomes in a blue and white braided bikini.

She drifted around and, in all the time I spent there, she never really seemed to do much of anything.

She didn't cook, for instance, because the Specks always seemed to eat the produce from the Big Rooster shop. In the packets.

When I was invited over for dinner occasionally we would sit around the table, open our takeaway boxes and tuck into the various dinner packs.

'Oh, a paradise pack,' cooed Helen and I knew exactly how Troy Lipson felt when she spoke those words.

As she went through the contents her father would bellow, 'For *Christ's* sake, eat that crumbed fried banana decently.'

'It's a banana fritter, Dad, that's what your menu says.'

'For Christ's sake, Helen, I don't care what it's called, eat it DECENTLY!'

He did have a point. It was hard not to stare as she went to work on the paradise pack's crumbed deep-fried banana. It was like a bad video clip mash-up of a Duran Duran and a Madonna song.

And now there was Helen and her little army of ghoulish pervs in the front garden. Mrs Speck might have been smiling benignly but I think my facial expression was more in line with the grubby gnomes, as I stood looking out the window at Helen while Karl was telling me something.

He had a soft voice — when he appealed for a wicket it was like a strangled groan — and it was incredibly hard to catch what he was saying. He spoke as if he were eating his words, getting half through them and then swallowing.

I didn't want to turn away from the Helen and Gnome show but Karl started tugging my arm.

I glanced at him and he said, 'D'y want see my chooks?' He said this so quietly I had to lean in.

I asked him what he meant.

He tugged my arm.

'*My* ch . . . . oo . . . . . . ks.'

'Your chickens?'

He nodded.

It seemed slightly odd that he would keep chickens, seeing as how the fridge was filled with chicken meat and his dad owned a Big Rooster outlet where he and his sister worked.

So I laughed.

Then I felt a bit ashamed because of the look on his face, so I pulled my eyes away from Helen.

'Yeah, sure I'd like to see your chooks.'

He smiled and we went out to the backyard where he showed me the pen that he had built and the chickens that were his pets.

He had names for them all that I could hardly hear as he softly mumbled them to me.

Then he picked one up that he mumbled was his favourite. It was a huge white thing with rather terrifying feet.

'She's called Cheryl.'

'Cheryl? You call her Cheryl?'

He smiled and nodded.

'She's special because she is blind,' he said softly.

'Blind?'

Karl nodded and showed me this unusual animal with white eyes.

He put it down and what I thought was a poor creature pecked about quite violently; in fact, it was lurching about. I suppose if you were a blind chook that is what you'd do. It bumped into another chicken, went ballistic, and pecked the other unfortunate animal and knocked it sideways. Then

Cheryl plodded around and settled herself in a fluffy ball of feathers.

I looked at Cheryl the blind chicken and then back up at Karl and said that she was a good chicken.

Karl smiled and said, 'I don't really like to show my chooks to many people.'

I nodded, and watching Cheryl the blind bully chicken, that made some sense.

We went back inside and ate some more takeaway chicken.

•

One holidays Karl invited me to the Specks' fishing shack on an island and when he told me that Helen was going as well I signed up eagerly.

We sat in the back of the Specks' Statesman – me, Karl and Helen. And Cheryl the blind chicken.

I sat by one window, Helen by another and in the middle was Karl with a large cardboard box in which Cheryl sat.

'For Christ's *sake*, Karl, I have no idea why you brought that bloody chicken.'

Nobody else was sure why either, but from what I could decipher from Karl's swallowed words he had brought Cheryl because she had been getting very rough with the other birds and he thought that it would be better if she went along with them on their holiday.

Mr Speck glowered, Mrs Speck smiled, Helen Speck stared out the window, I stared at her and Karl sat impassively with Cheryl clucking occasionally in the box.

The family's small fibro shack was fitted out well enough and was quite comfortable. It had its own generator which hummed away as we sat down to dinner with our Big Rooster dinner boxes.

Over the hum you could hear Cheryl occasionally give a muffled cluck or two.

And then the hum stopped.

And the lights went out.

It was dark. Very dark.

We sat for a bit and Mr Speck growled, 'For Christ's sake, that bloody thing. Fuel line on the genny's playing up. It'll be right in a minute.'

We sat for a while longer and then the hum started again and the lights came back on.

Then it stopped and the lights went off. Then it started again and the lights came on again.

It was like blinking your eyes a lot or flipping through one of those little pads filled with still images of a horse that runs as you flick the pages. Mr Speck looked more furious than ever and let out a great sigh when the hum stopped again and this time stayed dead.

'For Christ's *sake!*'

'God, Dad,' moaned Helen as we sat in complete darkness.

'Give it time,' said Mr Speck.

And then we heard Cheryl.

Buck-bucking. Very clearly. Not muffled.

'Karl, dear, is your little chicken out?' asked Mrs Speck.

Karl mumbled something and then Helen screamed.

'It pecked me! It pecked me!'

'For CHRIST'S SAKE!' roared Mr Speck. 'It's on the bloody table.'

And it was.

You could hear the chook walking slowly on the laminex table. Karl mumbled. Cheryl cluck-clucked quite loudly and Mr Speck roared.

I bumped into something and yelled and Helen cried out, 'What? What was that?'

'Me, I think,' I said and then, with some satisfaction, I thought that I had at last had some sort of fleeting physical contact with Helen Speck.

There was a hand on my arm and I thought it might have been hers.

I remembered that she was on the other side of the table.

'No, you dickhead, that!' she screamed.

'Helen, for Christ's sake, watch your language!' roared Mr Speck.

It was a case of timing more than anything else.

The hum started again, the lights came on and I saw Cheryl standing not far from Doug Speck's dinner box. Karl was impassive, Helen was rigid with fright and Mrs Speck was holding my hand. Smiling at me. Digging her nails into my hand with terror. I screamed and she screamed. Helen screamed. Karl stared and Mr Speck prepared to roar, sucking in a breath so violent that he looked like he would explode. And just before he did, the humming stopped.

The lights went out and Cheryl struck.

'My nose, for Christ's *sake*. My BLOODY nose.'

Then there was another scream, a huge squawk, the sounds of a struggle and Karl screaming in his swallowed manner. 'Leave Che . . . ryyyll 'lone!'

The lights came on and I saw Doug Speck and his son grappling and Cheryl helping herself to a paradise pack.

The generator behaved itself after that but was left to run for only as long as it took to clean up and re-box Cheryl. Then it was turned off and we got back into the Statesman and went home. I was dropped off outside my house, from where I waved goodbye to the Specks.

Even though I had the occasional fond thought of gnome shows, I didn't really see much of the Specks after that; they got on with their holidays and I got on with mine.

•

The next morning a few of us wandered along the beach as Ray and Delilah crept down low on the sand, then stalked and tried to herd two supremely disinterested Labradors. It was ridiculously entertaining: two stringy Kelpie puppies bobbing in and around the stout Labs that waddled along at their own pace like large pompous opera tenors.

There was a little girl standing not far away. She would have been about nine or ten. She watched a rock pool intently and then looked up at me.

'Are you the man who shows the films on his house?'

I nodded.

'Will you show the kangaroo tonight? Again?'

'That's the plan,' I said.

She looked worried.

'And you won't show any more toilet films?'

I smiled. 'No, not tonight.'

She nodded.

'Tonight it's a shark on the side of the house – a big one.'

She stared and then laughed.

'I love sharks.'

'All good people love sharks!'

'Except my brother. He's good but sharks scare him a bit.' She paused and thought. 'And the only thing he doesn't like more than sharks is toilets. But sharks are good.'

I nodded.

She ran back to where her brother and mother were.

'Sharkies, sharks on the house tonight!' she called out.

'But no donkey sausages,' said Niall.

The little girl stopped, and then burst out laughing.

'And no donkey sausages!'

Ray and Delilah continued to chase the two tenor Labradors and seagulls cried above.

It was that sort of holiday. Animals all around.

Other People's Holidays

It wasn't that the food was unpleasant or badly cooked; the caterer was usually very good and had been with the show for a long time. People liked him and he did the job with a minimum of fuss, even if he didn't wash his broccoli properly.

I liked him because he occasionally cooked chicken liver 'Greek style' and we used to chat about his days as a merchant marine engineer.

'How did you come to be catering for a television crew?' I asked him once as he barbecued the chicken liver.

'One of life's mysteries,' he said, smiling.

I asked him about another of life's mysteries. 'Why is it, Tim, that I have never found a hair of yours in anything you have ever cooked?' I asked. He was one of the hairiest cooks I had ever seen in my life

He smiled. 'One of life's mysteries.' He looked up from the hotplate and glanced out of the van. 'It'll be a mystery if anybody eats anything today.'

I nodded. That's why Hairy Tim was cooking my chicken inside his van, where he was going to allow me to eat it.

We were shooting on location just thirty minutes from the centre of Melbourne on what was one of the largest farms in the state.

The only problem was that it was a sewerage farm. So on a hot day like that day, no matter what you put out to eat, or when you put it out, within minutes flies and all sorts of odd flying things would swarm over it – if you didn't have the closed tarpaulin.

We didn't have the closed tarpaulin.

Instead, people had to sit where they could and eat as quickly as they could and then try to amuse themselves for the rest of the lunch break.

But on this day, Melbourne being Melbourne, as soon as the bug-covered food was taken away, the sky ripped apart in a storm that was as fierce as the day had been hot.

Everybody ran to find shelter, mostly under the groaning tarpaulin, which really wasn't keeping that many people dry.

That's why Gwen ran in to Hairy Tim's van where I was eating my Greek-style chicken livers.

Gwen was from the costume department and was very

nice. She wore Paddington Bear-style hats and flowing Laura Ashley skirts.

When she had had a few beers she would cut loose and do her favourite party trick, an impersonation of Fozzie Bear from the Muppets.

One of the directors first met her when she was doing this particular impersonation and thought, in his words, 'That she was a bit simple,' and whenever he spoke to her he raised his voice and spoke slowly.

Gwen was a rigorous vegetarian, despite the fact her father was a butcher and her mother was the daughter of a butcher. In fact, most of her uncles also seemed to be butchers and her brothers were both butchers. She looked at the meal I was polishing off.

'Oh, great,' she said. 'It's pissing down, all the other actors are getting drenched and I'm in an enclosed space with a carnivore.'

'Well, it could be worse,' said Hairy Tim, pointing at me. 'He could be having the fly-blown mixed grill that was on offer at lunch. At least you're only dealing with one piece of dead animal.'

Gwen smiled. 'True, it could be a lot worse. It's good to remember that.'

'Got anything to draw on, Gwen, in the "could be a lot worse" department?' asked Hairy Tim. Before she could answer, we all jumped as an explosion of thunder roared above and hail started to fall.

It only lasted for a few minutes but we were all silent; no use trying to talk when it's so noisy.

When the hail stopped and the rain began to lighten, Gwen turned back to us. 'Nothing could be worse than my first holiday overseas. Contiki.'

'Contiki?' asked Hairy Tim.

'Oh yeah,' said Gwen. 'Saved up working in Woolies and wanted to go overseas before I went to uni. I was too scared to go by myself so I went on a Contiki bus tour to Europe.'

A New Zealander who wanted to travel through Europe invented Contiki tours in the 1960s. He bought a bus, collected some people and created a fairly profitable business. The customers were aged between eighteen and thirty-five, the youth market.

'My brother said the tours were great,' said Gwen,

'But your brother is a butcher, right?' said Hairy Tim.

Gwen nodded. 'I knew I shouldn't have trusted the bastard,' and she laughed.

'Not much chop?'

'Yes, well, it was an experience. Once you got over being excited about being in Europe, seeing all that stuff, you suddenly were experiencing the other travellers.'

According to Gwen, her fellow Contikians were nearly all at the higher end of the Contiki age register and looked like they all came from the same family.

'Honestly, I have never seen so many cream cardigans in my life. They were all angry Presbyterians from New Zealand.

Too much meat.' Gwen shuddered and pointed at me, 'The things I saw in the toilet on that bus — they would break you.

'The angry Presbyterians started grumbling about the song that we had to sing every day.'

On the tours, a theme song was played to create the right mood. In Gwen's case it was 'I Feel Good' — but there was some resistance to it.

'When the tour guide played the tour song, these guys would sing "Ten Guitars".'

'Oh, now that's a great song,' said Hairy Tim.

'It is,' I added. 'Vegetarians and meat-eaters can agree on that one.'

'Well, maybe on another bus,' said Gwen. 'These guys sang it really quietly, like some weird chant, underneath the rest of us.'

'So they were on a different tour?'

'Basically, yeah — half the bus just wanted to get wasted and this lot were wanting to do all the sightseeing, eat as much meat as they could and sing "Ten Guitars". I got really drunk a couple of times and this one angry cardigan guy with odd-coloured eyes — like David Bowie — who was almost good-looking but who would sing the chorus of "Ten Guitars" a bit louder every day, started trying to talk to me more.'

'Don't tell me,' said Hairy Tim. 'He was a —'

'Butcher!' shrieked Gwen above the rain. 'He was a butcher and I got really drunk one night and I spoke to him about all the cuts of meat and how to cut and hang meat. We even talked about how to scour lamb flaps to get more out of the roll. He thought it was love.'

'How did it pan out?'

'When we got to Rome, we went out to a restaurant and he ordered some tripe for me and we sat looking at each other over this steaming tripe, me looking into his odd-coloured eyes, poor sod. I had a few drinks and starting talking like Fozzie Bear and he started trying to talk like the characters from the *Muppet Show*. His best was Beaker. Although Animal and Gonzo were pretty good. So yeah, there are worse places I could be.'

We all shivered at the thought. Gwen's Fozzie Bear and the angry cardigan with the odd-coloured eyes meeping like Beaker, the perennially agitated cone-headed laboratory assistant, over a bowl of offal.

'We even sent Christmas cards to each other for a while – his were from his butcher's shop. You know those ones that small businesses get printed up? They come out with a bit of holly in one corner and a smiling pig with an apple in its mouth and a happy butcher wearing an apron. And he always wrote "I'll never forget our Contiki time." Bizarre.'

The rain faded enough to start shooting again and, as we stepped down from Hairy Tim's van, Gwen said, 'Back to real life.'

It wasn't the first time I had heard holidays being separated from the rest of your life.

'Aren't holidays real life too?' I asked, and she turned to me, laughing.

'Not for me, holidays are the icing on the cake. My real life is dealing with hams like you!'

•

Finding out about other people's holidays is oddly revealing, not only for the person who is telling you about them but also about yourself.

For a long time, I never thought of there being a demarcation point between real life and holidays, which goes to show how lucky a life I had been leading and just how far up my bum my head must have been.

Holidays are that period of time when people may be truer to themselves than they are when they're in the middle of their 'real life'. Or maybe they're not.

A building inspector I knew didn't have the happiest of countenances. It wasn't that he was devoid of humour or a pleasant nature, it's just that dealing with people who expected the worst from him had taken a few strips of happiness off his personality veneer.

'Lugubriously sceptical' would best describe the quality he brought to his conversation and I could see that he looked gloweringly lugubrious as he stomped up towards my front door to check on some renovations.

'Hello, Geoff,' I said as happily as I could.

He grunted a hello.

'How've you been travelling?'

He stopped and looked at me as if he were trying to work out whether what I was saying was loaded in any way.

'You right?'

He nodded and grunted again.

'Yeah, sorry, I thought you might have been having a go.'

'Why?'

He groaned. 'Just come back from holiday.'

'Where to?'

He looked like he wanted to spit. 'Europe. Went to Italy, France, Austria, Germany – went all over.'

'No good?'

He looked straight at me. 'Not much good, no.'

The problem, it seemed, was that his mother-in-law had gone along. And nothing was on time, which was made worse because his mother-in-law couldn't keep up and was always getting lost.

'And all she wanted to do was to see the bloody buildings, I mean I was supposed to be on holiday and she wants to inspect stuff.'

The Italians got all the bookings mixed up and nobody seemed to care. He had to spend a week sharing a hotel room with his wife and her mother. Then in Belgium their bags didn't turn up and in France everything was dirty and nobody seemed to care.

'The French were worse than the Italians because they made you feel like it was your fault when they stuffed up; the Italians just didn't care what you thought.'

I started feeling a bit nervous about how he'd treat the renovation works that were under way.

'But Germany would have been okay?'

Unbelievably he smiled.

'Thank Christ for the Krauts. Fantastic. Everything organised, booked my mother-in-law on a cruise and an art tour. The food was great; loved the food. Clean and lots of mustard. And lots of bands there. Musical bands – they were terrific. Everything on time. Ticked all the boxes – Austria nearly as good, just that there was too much cheese. But apart from that, they were the standouts, made it all worthwhile.'

His mood lifted as he had a fairly cursory glance at the renovation. 'You know, they didn't try and be clever, didn't try and be smart or cool. Just did their jobs. Ticked every box.'

He gave a cheery wave when he left, and let us know that the 'renos' were fine.

'It's good to get away, you know,' he said. 'Good to have the good times stored up in the memory bank, gets you through the day.'

•

Sometimes in the course of earning a dollar by pretending to be somebody else the demarcation line between holidays and real life can become a bit blurred for me.

On one occasion I was working away from home on a television series and was housed in what was more or less a resort during a peak holiday period. The job wasn't going along that smoothly and at night in the bar you could easily tell the difference between people having a drink to top off a pleasant day of relaxing and those who needed the almost medicinal glass to calm down after running around like mad things.

'You're working on that film thing, aren't you?' A sunburnt tourist smiled up at me.

I nodded.

'Yes, I thought so. I can tell by the way you all drink so quickly. At first I thought it was an Australian thing but the barman said that you were all working on some film and that's why you drink the way you do.'

'And how's that?' I said, looking at the glass I'd just polished off.

'Well, you all drink like Dr Jekyll drinking an antidote to shoo off Mr Hyde. You know, quick and desperate, like your hand's shaking when it's not.'

'Well, mate, I can see you've been giving this a bit of thought,' I said.

He nodded. 'Yeah, not much else to do except have a bit of a sit and a look-see on the way to FUBAR Land.'

I asked him what and where FUBAR Land was.

'Fucked Up Beyond All Recognition Land. The only other people who drink like us holiday-makers, the bar guy said, were rugby league players.'

There were a lot of families around as well, tourists to FUBAR Land, and one family in particular caught my eye.

They had colonised an area by one of the pools and had conquered all comers to claim the big banana lounges in a spot where the sun and the shade were just the right mix.

The father was sent down early in the morning to drape towels, books, hats and bags around the banana lounges to stake the claim and then he would disappear, to be replaced by one of the children and eventually the mother.

Then they would gather by the good corner of the pool and relax. This followed a set routine of the father and mother enjoying the banana lounges and reading their books, large door-stopping blocks of pulped tree – 'holiday reads'.

They never seemed to communicate much with each other, or anybody else for that matter, save for the occasional, 'Dominiiiiiiiiic! Gentle,' or 'Brodiiiiiiiiiiiiiie, gentle,' and then, 'Stop IIIIIIIIIT!' which I think was a general direction of behaviour to both of their sons.

And as for Dominiiiiiiiiic and Brodiiiiiiie, they prowled about the pool trying to inflict merry hell upon each other.

Cain and Abel at the deep and shallow end. Almost every water activity they embarked upon was an excuse to try to pummel each other in as many ways as possible and with an almost biblical fury.

And all the while the parents would be reading their 'holiday reads', *Fifty Shades of Grey* for her and some action adventure muscle-builder for him.

The mother read the book impassively, occasionally looking up at a splash and a scream in the water and then glancing up into the blue sky, watching no discernible thing.

Fifty Shades of Grey.

Permissible porn. Escapist entertainment. The book had been on sale in almost every possible outlet, the roadhouse down the road had copies and even Coles had piles under 'holiday specials'. And at both the roadhouse and at Coles, lad mags covered with bikini-clad women were stacked not far from the piles of *Fifty Shades of Grey*.

As the woman by the pool read the book with that impassive intensity, I saw what it was her partner was grazing on and engrossed in: fifty different ways to kill people with a Matthew Reilly thriller.

Good escapist fun? One couldn't begin to imagine what happened in their part of the family unit after lights out. And whose business was it really? They were on holiday.

One night when I had returned to the resort in the early evening after a day's work and had downed a couple of medicinal Dr Jekyll and Mr Hydes, I was on my way to my room when I heard a noise in the pool.

I stopped and saw the banana lounge colonisers not far from 'their' corner.

The mother and father stood arm in arm and were laughing, really gut-busting happy laughter.

Their two boys, Dominiiiiiiiiiic and Brodiiiiiiiie, had developed some pool trick where one would lift the other up on their shoulders and then launch them somersaulting in the air. And the somersaulter would dive into the pool and then lift his brother up into the air and repeat the whole process.

A bus tour group of old Germans bobbed on the other side of the pool applauding. Some in floating rings and on li-los.

The boys were laughing in between gulps of air.

I looked for a bit and then turned back and went on to my room, the sounds of other people's holidays echoing after I'd closed the door.

•

There are some lonely places in the world but one of the loneliest would have to be a hotel room by yourself with the television your only company and the sound of other people's holidays outside.

The feeling usually hits just after you've rung your family. You hang up and feel not quite right. Not where you should be. So you sit. On a bed with sheets made up like the strait-jacket on some crazed lunatic from an old movie. It's a major operation in logistics to unlock the bed, but the de-sheeting will come later; now you're tired from travel and from what passes as work.

Lying on a bed, not tempted by the treats of the mini bar – for the idea that exorbitantly priced little bottles and tiny portions could ever be treats seems crazy – invariably, you switch on the television.

I have never been able to see the point of watching in-house movies – you usually have to pay the equivalent amount to the cinema version and all you get is a squashed screen. And the in-house porn, always politely termed 'adult channels', is too sad for words.

A younger friend of mine once told me that in-house porn was 'nostalgically twentieth century'. 'That's what a laptop is for,' he added.

He's young – but the idea of pornography being an item of nostalgia is a little bizarre.

But then, why not? Nostalgia is what television in a hotel room is all about as you surf through the vast digital trash and treasure of the airwaves.

What would the cable history channels have done without World War II?

Or generic extreme adventurers in neat natty outdoor clothes wrestling crocodiles or surviving off the land?

I'd like to see Bear Grylls have a crack at surviving a lonely hotel room – him against the bed sheets and the mini bar.

Or there's the incessant replays of sporting channels. You feel your age when you see old football matches you remember being at. Only all the players seem to have funny haircuts, and look smaller and less swollen.

The commentators screech just as melodramatically and every moment is the same and as special as the game that was played only a week ago. Life seems like a hamster wheel.

You're just not in the mood. You lie in bed and switch the television to the radio channels.

Now this is a wasteland that makes T. S. Eliot's look like verdant rainforest.

Late-night talkback or love song dedications.

The talk show is especially enjoyable in a tortured way because the poor old sod that's on can't get anybody to ring up and chat so he goes on and on and on.

Suddenly you are tempted to ring him up. You look at the phone and realise there's a reason why nobody is ringing in to chat. He's a barking, lonely old voice in the night.

I realise I'm not that lonely. I lie there and think of how much I like my friends. How much I love my family, the one I grew up with and the one I have now. I switch the noise off and drift off to sleep.

Sometimes the best place to realise what you've got is the loneliest place.

The next day as I walked past the pool, I saw that the banana lounges in the 'good corner' were unattended, no books or towels or bags draped proprietorially over them. I supposed the colonising family had disappeared. Back to real life. And I supposed that very soon their place would be taken by other people.

The pool was quiet. I went to work.

•

The first time I met Kaye it wasn't that long after my family and I had started going down to the Mornington Peninsula and a little village for extended holidays. The place consisted of some wetlands, a school camp down by the beach, an overly energetic foreshore committee, lots of trees and a series of unsealed dirt roads.

It was quiet and only ever came alive for a couple of weeks a year during the school holidays.

In a strange way it was similar to the Redcliffe Peninsula

in that it was a bay beach and the residents, like Kaye, lived there while other people would spend their holidays there.

Kaye had seen a fair amount of holiday-makers in this little town. Her father was one of the founders of the yacht club and she'd watched as the cottages were gradually turned into more substantial holiday dwellings.

Little houses still dotted the area but many were being renovated or demolished to make way for grander holiday visions.

When she'd finished helping out at the general store, Kaye would wander around saying hello to half the patrons, which was always a good way to catch up with anything that had happened in the area, or a chance to have a chat.

One time, I asked her what was news.

'I'm off to Mongolia,' she said. 'Inner and Outer! Boom, boom!'

I asked why.

'A holiday, you boofhead. A friend is going off on a tour and somebody couldn't make it so I've put my hand up – so Mongolia, here we come.'

'Do you always go away for your holidays from here?'

She laughed. 'Well, of course not. How many times do I see you down here?'

It was true. I nearly always made a point of coming down on weekends and holidays and, more often than not, Kaye would always pop up. If not at the general store with its collection of dogs tied out the front and the clutch of parked strollers, then perhaps at the hall by the tennis courts as she emerged fresh from a yoga class. I even remember once having an hour-long conversation about dog bones with her in the supermarket in town, five minutes up the road. It was over the Christmas–New Year holidays when conversations could take ages because time just seemed to doze. It began with the question of which sized dog bones would suit our manic Kelpies, then drifted off into whether it's best to get the supermarket bones or the ones from the butchers and then into why it's so marvellous that you never see any unhappy butchers.

'It's kind of sweet in a flesh-tearing way, isn't it?' said Kaye. 'They're just always so bloody happy.'

Then we chatted about the latest 'big house' that was being built down at the little village where I spent so much time and where Kaye lived.

'Well, the block of land is big enough, so it doesn't really matter. It's when they try to squeeze a McMansion on a small block that it all goes pear-shaped.'

It always surprised me a bit that Kaye, who was so of this little place by the coast, would travel so far away on her holidays when she chose to take one.

'It's because this place is so beautiful, you boofhead. If I'm going to get away from here, I have to really go away Big!'

'So that's why you head overseas when you go?' I asked.

'Well, I go because I want to find new horizons and get away from the routine you usually have, the responsibilities that bind you, and if you can't enjoy that then I don't know what you could enjoy. I can tell you this: there's is nothing like coming home. Never once have I not wanted to come back to this place.'

She pointed a finger gently at me. 'You know, I've bumped into people all over the world who've been here – met a man in Italy who used to deliver Coca-Cola to this general store. And on the Tube in London, this youngish fellow came up to me as he was getting off and I thought, what's this? He smiled and said, "Say hello to the yacht club for me!" and he was on his way. Must have been working over there.'

She looked around at the crowded store and smiled. 'People come here, but you know time rolls along and the kids want to go away to the surf – it's just people growing up. Getting on and moving away.'

A little boy staggered past on his way to the toilet with a worried-looking father in tow. 'I'm buuuusting!' the kid yelled, half laughing.

Kaye clicked her fingers. 'Now there's a collection of holiday images for you – toilets! My god, you don't know how blessed we are in this country.'

Toilets, it seems, are another world.

'In Spain, a lot of the toilets are stand up and you have to put your feet either side and aim, do your best to be a real Annie Oakley. And then in Russia, the smell of the place – you just have to make do in the bush.'

There was a cry from the toilets and then the little boy yelled out, 'Such a lot of wee in me!'

The father walked back behind the boy. 'Just a stage he's going through – all a bit of a novelty for him at the moment.'

Kaye smiled. 'That a boy,' and then she turned back to me. 'I'll tell you what's a novelty – the Czar's Palace in Leningrad, better than the scenic railway at Luna Park! All you could see was this fog of yellow pea soup and you go in on these starting block things and hang and hover.'

'Hang and Hover sounds like a ride at Luna Park.'

'Well, this one was a beauty. You're in a position where you see over the door – the things were so high and you'd hang there on this bit of rope and hover over the toilet and do your business. But the rope was the door lock, so you had to hang onto it to keep the door closed and to hold yourself in position. It's not good when you're – what did that little fellow say? When you're buuuuuusting!'

She shivered when she remembered how she had to flush the thing and get off quick before the water slushed around her feet. 'You had to pay, too; unbelievable. Well, you used to have to pay for the Collins Street toilets, I suppose. The Bizarre Czar they could call it.' She laughed.

'What?'

'The toilet ride at Luna Park – the Bizarre Czar!'

Kaye had more holiday ablution tales.

'I must have been the only person ever to go to India and get constipated, you know. My mother couldn't believe it but I knew how it happened. I went to an ashram and clenched myself during meditation because I didn't want to get bitten by a mozzie – so many over there, you know – and when you meditate you use all the muscles you've got. And then some you borrow off the bank.'

She let out a laugh. 'Well, it's a theory, anyway. And I made up for it all with Mexico. My god, I went into this restaurant to get away from all the flies and ordered fish, absolutely delicious, and half an hour later it's the New Year's fireworks. Monty's revenge like nobody's business.'

She was referring to the colloquial term for any cases of traveller's diarrhoea caught during a visit to Mexico.

Monty, or Montezuma to be more formal, was an Aztec ruler who was slaughtered by Hernán Cortés's conquistadors.

Kaye's connection with Monty was a long way from her first holiday.

This first holiday she went on was when she was in her early twenties and it was all because of her boyfriend.

'He went to Queensland for a holiday and then, when he came back, I of course wanted to spend time with him but he buggered off and went to Shepparton. So I thought, if he's off to Shep then blow him. I got a bit peeved, I don't mind telling you, and just got up and went and booked a passage on this Italian ocean liner called the *Galileo* and off I went.'

'How long for?'

'Working holiday for two years!' She shook her head. 'And this lovely dill of a boy comes back and asks why I'm going and I said, "Because you went off to Shep," and he says, "Well, all you had to do was ask and you could have come."'

She rolled her eyes. 'Should have seen us when I left. He was on the wharf with this shiny scarf and I waved for what seemed like hours. Slow farewells are hard, you know.'

And then she got seasick. When she got over that she decided that travelling alone was fun.

'When you're alone, it doesn't mean you're lonely. That's something people should find out for themselves, you know. Oh, it can be a bit off when you go out for dinner by yourself but being by yourself makes you talk to people. To meet them, however you meet them – there's nobody else there whispering in your ear or to be frightened with. I like it.'

Travelling by herself made Kaye trust what she calls her feelings. 'Or your instincts, if you like, and you know them well after a while. They're different from being a bit shy or tentative, there's a real unease you get. As though it's some sort of traveller's sense.'

Kaye tells me another story about Mexico.

'I got up and things didn't feel right. I walked outside for a bit but it felt, I don't know – all odd and unsettled. Wasn't traveller's tiredness, but that sense.'

She waited for the reception to open and booked another ticket off to Oaxaca, which was a handcraft and weaving area by the coast.

'It was perfect, apart from another round of Monty's revenge, but I could deal with that. And it wasn't like the hotel I had moved from burnt down or was filled with ghosts and whatnot – it just wasn't right for me and I knew it.'

Two young girls, I guess sisters, crouched down on the general store's verandah where we were seated, and watched some ants crawling amongst a few small pieces of dropped food.

'Where are you going, anty ant?' said one young girl.

We watched them and then Kaye said, 'All their lives in front of them – wonder where they'll go?'

'Any advice for them?' I asked.

Kaye smiled. 'Last person to ask advice from is me, but I suppose there's a few tips that might come in handy. Get a good pair of sandals; good old-fashioned ones with cushioning if you go walking in Europe – all those cobbles play havoc with your joints. Try not to drink the water, no matter how much it may upset the locals – the Greeks were the worst, and I'm telling you, you could strip varnish with some of the stuff that came out of those taps over there. As soon as you said anything they'd be at you! Hang on to the rope tightly on the Bizarre Czar!'

She laughed again. 'You know, there's something about the air here,' she said, indicating the town. 'Something that just makes things so clear. Those young girls watching the anty ants, I hope they never lose that curiosity, their wonder at things; that's the best thing they could do.'

We said goodbye. Me to mooch along the beach and Kaye to pack for Mongolia. Inner and Outer, here she comes.

As I wandered away, I thought that listening to other people's holidays is a little like a conversational lucky dip. You can be bored witless or, when you chat with someone like Kaye, feel like you've almost been there yourself.

From the Bizarre Czar to Monty's Revenge and the Hang and over, she took me to places where I don't think I'd otherwise ever go, literally – a virtual around the world ladies' toilet tour.

But I also thought how nice it would be to be on a holiday, somewhere out there, and to bump into Kaye and be reminded of this beautiful little village by the sea. And, knowing Kaye, that is exactly what will happen in Mongolia, Inner and Outer.

·

I met my friend Willis in drama school and it was fair to say that he liked to think of himself as a passable cross between David Bowie and Lou Reed, while I even more tragically still held out a vague dream of being selected in the second row for the Wallabies. Well, we all have our secret dreams.

I have known Willis for nearly thirty years and, of course, during that time you can't help but change and have bits and pieces of you knocked off and burnished by life.

Yet Willis seems not to have changed and has kept up his habits and manner of living. In particular, his rather haphazard approach of letting the universe, or 'Whatever it is you want to call what's out there: fate, karma, destiny or blind-arsed luck' as he puts it, determine his life.

Once when he was into numerology he saw a girl walking along the street and they smiled at each other. He thought that perhaps if she walked past five cars and turned back then maybe, perhaps, they were meant to be.

It was a five sort of day. He waited and counted and she turned back and came and spoke to him. They were together for nearly a year and a half.

It turned out, however, that her stopping didn't have much to do with numerology; she was pissed as a newt and was trying to find her car.

She was as close a thing to a functioning alcoholic as you could get, except no alcoholic ever really functions that well. And she could never really work out why she and Willis were together.

'Well, you know, sometimes it's hard to tell between destiny and blind-pissed circumstance. But she was a nice girl,' Willis said with a smile.

It was this habit of letting things fall where they may that made his holidays so interesting.

Usually he would get a ticket to wherever he wanted and just go. Once, he toured, of all places, Afghanistan shortly before the attacks of September 11.

He and a German traveller, Jorg, who he had hooked up with, tried to grow beards to blend in with the locals. Although why a local would be wearing a David Bowie *Diamond Dogs* t-shirt is anyone's guess.

'Jorg would get upset every morning because his beard was just facial fuzz and he'd look at me and see that my whiskers were getting a hurry on and he'd get all grumpy. First of all, with his fuzz on his chin, he'd slap at his cheeks and say in this German accent, "Koom on, koom on, fugt you. Fugging hair grow, fugging." Then he'd start swearing at me in this weird mixture of German and English about me being a hairy pixie bastardy fugger.'

Travelling by bus, the two would be laughed at by what Willis took to be the local Taliban. They'd point at the two travellers' beards and make 'girly' gestures with their hands.

'It was sort of scary but was made worse because Jorg thought they were giving us some sort of greeting, so he'd start hello-ing in this amplified German style and then the Taliban would get curious and sometimes a bit annoyed. Which would set Jorg off. Quite stressful.

'It was amazing nothing really bad happened to us. But whether it was fun or not, I don't know. In India there was this great divide between poor – people were beyond poor – and the guys who had stuff, but I never saw bodies hanging from trees like in Afghanistan. And all these guys and their manly beards with guns. Awful. But then I don't know, I never learnt that much about what was going on. I thought it would be cool to just pass through. Better watch out what you wish for.'

Willis's holidays were always thrown together and had a 'let's see what happens' quality that should really have been marketed to a broader audience. Willis's 'What will be, will be' Tours.

He had a series of exotic cars that he bought and somehow ran into the ground pursuing some recreational wanderlust. All his cars were given names; a little Fiat was called the Spick mobile and another Hillman Minx was deemed the Danger mobile. A Cortina that he called Augustus, for no apparent reason other than it sounded vaguely noble, came to grief when he was driving down to the southwest of Western Australia and was engaged in a duel with a man driving a Monaro.

Just how this duel took place I don't know but Willis proudly told me that, before the regal little Augustus Cortina cooked itself with some help from his heavy right foot, he had passed the Monaro, which had been pulled over by the police for speeding.

'I gave him an up-yours victory beep and then the poor thing just died. Pushed it into a garage and sold Augustus for 150 dollars.'

He then rang up the caravan park I was staying at and asked if my girlfriend and I could come and pick him and his girlfriend up.

We did and then he and his girlfriend camped quite happily in the shower block of the caravan park.

'What sort of person sleeps in a shower block?' asked my girlfriend at the time, who was a lovely woman and destined for greater things in life than me. She didn't like leaving things unplanned or to chance.

'Willis does, and I bet you any money he's having a ball.'

And of course he was.

Willis's car holidays never got any better. Years later when he had met a lovely woman and they had a beautiful little girl together he decided that it would be grand if they went off to a music festival in southern Victoria.

His car, an old Mitsubishi called Mitsy, crapped out in the middle of nowhere, which luckily wasn't that far from where the festival was held.

It began raining and the family of three hitchhiked in the wet until somebody picked them up and drove them to a pub. Here Willis decided to trust country hospitality and asked around the bar for a good mechanic.

The country heads asked Willis where Mitsy had broken down.

Willis told them.

A country head said he would take a look at it tomorrow. Willis asked if he should get a tow. The country head said the car wouldn't be going anywhere. 'She'll be right.'

The next day, Willis hitched a lift with the country head mechanic and pulled up next to a prone Mitsy.

Willis got out and glanced at Mitsy. She was up on blocks with her four wheels missing.

'Looks like your car's out of petrol and needs a new starter. I can fix that up for you now. What a fluke to have just what you need in the back of me truck,' said the country head.

Willis nodded and didn't say anything about the wheels until the country head was done with his work underneath Mitsy's bonnet.

'Should be right now,' said the country head.

Willis looked at Mitsy. 'What about my wheels?'

'Yeah, bit of a problem, that,' said the country head sagely. 'But you're in luck, matey – I've got a set that should do just right. Retreads.'

'Where?'

'Well, would you believe that they're in the back of the truck?'

Willis was pretty certain that the tyres were the same ones Mitsy had had on when the holiday to the music festival started.

'He hadn't even cleaned them, which in hindsight I think was a bit poor. There was still a vague outline of a parking mark from some traffic ranger scratched on the driver's side front wheel. I mean, if you're going to go to all that effort you might as well present a bit better.'

I asked Willis what he did.

'Oh, well, you know, we all have to live. He could have been an almost psychic mechanic who happened to have all the stuff that was needed to fix Mitsy. I'll go with that explanation, I think – more romantic.'

And he laughed.

I asked his partner what she thought of all the kerfuffle concerning their trip to the music festival. She laughed as hard as Willis and said, 'Just another day in the journey.'

•

I had a director who once began a play I was appearing in with what he called a statement of intent and a statement of desire. 'Journeys,' he said loudly and then repeated in a dramatic soft stage whisper, 'journeys.'

He smiled at us, nodded his head and carried on. 'Journeys have a beginning and an end and when the urge to take a journey takes hold of you, then there is nothing that can prevent us from embarking on that journey. Let's embark and soar on this journey.' Then he gathered the cast and the crew in a circle, we all held hands and hummed 'Somewhere Over the Rainbow'. Which, come to think of it, was an odd choice of song for a surrealistic play set in an Italian theatre company about life and death and dreams.

The poor sod had something of a breakdown in the second week of rehearsal. It was brought on by a woman who, when asked to shout faster, spoke slower and it led to one of the most immortal bits of direction ever given: 'Oh Christ, if that's how you want to do it, suit yourself, dear.'

The words of the breakdown director seemed a bit indulgent at the time, but it's true that sometimes the urge to take a particular holiday, or journey, can be so strong that it can't be resisted.

A friend of mine called Alison took the plunge on a holiday that she never thought she'd ever embark upon.

She's a casting agent and making a living in the business of film and television casting can be quite a draining thing to do with your life. It means being on the front line of dealing with actors, all their expectations and fears of rejection, and at the same time juggling the whims of directors, the needs of producers and the demands of television networks, theatre or production companies.

In many ways, you can't really win and it's a profession from which a break and a holiday do the world of good.

In the holiday stakes Alison is certainly no slouch. Mexico, America, dog-sledding in Canada, volcano-watching in the Hainan islands and reef-diving in the South Pacific are all notches she has marked off on her holiday list.

But, for as long as she could remember, Alison had dreamt of travelling solo with a dog.

It sounds like a concept for a television show, but there is a rich history, both in fact and fiction, of such travels.

'I have romanticised the idea forever,' Alison said. 'My hero is Emily Carr – a Canadian painter who travelled through British Columbia and the West Islands during 1898 and onwards, usually with her dog and a horse or on foot. She was unconventional, strong, clever and passionate about her country and her art.'

Emily Carr made her dog a backpack so that it could carry her painting boards, brushes and paints. Her life had been fairly unadventurous, but then she started to travel. She loved the Canadian landscape and discovered that the culture of the Indigenous peoples in many ways matched her own ideas about art and life.

'She was a woman who wasn't afraid to say, "I am going to have a go at living the life I want to lead. Despite whatever anybody says." And that type of woman,' said Alison, 'is worth her weight in gold.'

So many people are told they can't do things because of who and what they are. Because of their age, race, religion or gender.

But Carr was just one of Alison's reasons for being keen on becoming a solo female traveller with hound. Her library is full of books about people who built their own log cabins in Alaska; people who walked the wild trails of America; those who run across the world, living with the basics; those who drop off the grid and live without money or the want of anything. Ideally, they all have a dog with them; mostly, they do.

'There are so many when I think about them.' And she rattled them off like family members. *'Tracks, Woodswoman, A Walk in the Woods, Wild, My First Summer in the Sierra, Travels with Charley* – that old souse Steinbeck and I have a love affair – *Call of the Wild* and on and on.'

Why she hadn't done this earlier she wasn't sure, but she had finally committed to the idea.

'The timing was right, I had the funds to buy myself a reliable van, a dog entered my life, Hunter or H Man, who really is the ultimate camp dog. He's brave, small – being compact is so underrated it's not funny – and he's attuned to me and has those characteristics I needed, and he was adventurous and loving.

'And finally, I put aside the voices over the years that told me all the negatives, the voices of men and women (mainly men) who expressed their concern about my safety and openly questioned my ability. I put aside the voices that talked of loneliness. And I made plans. I drew maps and in my mind I drew pictures.'

She took two weeks off from dealing with the casting of make-believe dramas and adventures, and cast herself in her own story. She dipped her toe in, wanting to see if she could do her adventure holiday and, more importantly, to find out if she liked it.

In some ways, that was the biggest risk of all because turning a dream into reality can be fraught with all sorts of calamity. But she knew that if she did like it, she had the rest of her life to continue the journey.

She began the holiday with her partner Richard and Hunter out on a weekend at Ninety Mile Beach near Lakes Entrance. They built a big fire, drank wine and, as any caring and loving partner would do, Richard went over the maps she had prepared for the trip again. Then he checked the dual battery system and went over and over all the equipment.

And then there was one last thing for him to do.

'Richard toasted me and told me he loved me and on the Sunday he drove home and the H Man and I drove off for our first night alone together, further up along the Ninety Mile Beach.'

For those two weeks, Alison and Hunter moved every two days, in some places only staying a night.

'I had to make decisions on where to stay alone. I had limited choices due to the H Man being with me.' This meant staying true to Alison's idea of being a solo female traveller.

'I didn't want to stay in a caravan park. And in a 25-year-old diesel Toyota urban van I managed to cover about 2000 kilometres in Gippsland. It made a bit of a racket but it didn't really seem to matter that much. We went from the beach to Lake Tyers then up the Snowy Mountains and over to Dargo and finally to a forest where I sat alone, and as the darkness descended you could feel the trees move closer.'

For someone who worked in a business that made so much noise about what it did and what it was going to do, Alison found this a relief.

'I found out that I enjoy silence. I enjoy a long departure from the chattering troupes. And that I was comfortable as I shed any vestiges of my city life, washing in rivers, making my own fires, eating simple and tasteless food and having no plans but being comfortable with the course of each day.'

Each part of the holiday opened up new possibilities. 'I took photos of birds. I had bought myself a good camera and tripod before I left, and I would sit and wait for the perfect shot of gracious and mournful black cockatoos. I revelled in the bird life.'

The great joy of her adventure was never knowing what was going to happen, that each day she would have to sift through whatever information she could gather. This embracing of uncertainty was a welcome surprise.

'I never knew that would happen.'

And she had better luck than Willis with wells of wisdom. 'I learned that the local pub was always a good place to start for advice on camping.'

But she confronted some expected obstacles. 'I held fast at Lake Tyers as men with more fish in their hand than teeth in their mouth told me I was a silly girl, and to watch out for the arseholes that are out there. You could really spot them a mile away. Sometimes cliché is sadly just too accurate. I recoiled from dead roos dumped unceremoniously in the bush by hunters with no respect. I marvelled at the prehistoric goannas, larger than my dog. And all this left me feeling wonderful. I felt young and truly free.'

That didn't mean everything went to an ordered holiday timetable. Her nerves were tested when she unknowingly drove her two-wheel drive van along what she eventually realised was a four-wheel drive track for thirty long minutes. Long minutes because she was driving along the mountain peaks of the Snowy, which were too narrow for her to comfortably turn around, when she realised she was in strife.

'I knew I was in trouble, but it takes a few moments to really see the difficulties and the danger you're in. Then it hits and I understand that my tyres skidding along the loose rocks is real and that my adventure has this threat attached.

'And just when it seems to be too awful, you get through it. I finished up coming upon one of the most beautiful mountain beaches I've ever seen, the sand fine and yellow, the mountains stood there like some – well, the way mountains are supposed to be, godlike.

'The water was cold and crystal clear. Beautiful. But I don't mind admitting that I had been scared. Scared of being on a road that I wasn't supposed to be on and being alone.

'But the wonderful thing was that I had Hunter with me and to see at the end of that long awful thirty minutes this beauty. I cried. I cried at the sheer splendour of it all.'

Alison came home proud of what she had done, thrilled with the knowledge that she too was brave, like the heroes and heroines in the books that she had read. It's not often that any of us get to achieve something like that in life and do it not only on our terms but those of the people and the characters who have inspired us.

To live that holiday relying on her own skill and prowess, but also with the companionship of her dog, might sound like something out of a film she was trying to cast, but it added another level to her trip to be sharing it with her dog, Hunter.

'And my dog. Ahhh, my dog. Each night it felt good to have my dog next to me, curling up to sleep with his head heavy on my legs and his silly ears available for stroking. He was a very patient and delightful travelling companion. With little to complain about, no arguments and very few needs, he made me feel safe, as despite his size he can roar at an approaching stranger with the lungs of a lion.'

She looked no further than John Steinbeck to find the perfect way of describing that holiday where she had lived as a solo girl traveller with her dog. Just as Steinbeck wrote in *Travels with Charley* she thought that, 'Between the war of reality and romance, reality is not the stronger'.

It's when you hear about other people's holidays that those words ring true, because they accept the proposition of real life being what a person does at work and holidays being a romance of the soul.

At the same time, how can the two lives be separated?

For like any romance, those holidays are carried within your memory. When Alison tells people about that holiday, she feels like thanking them for asking about it because she revisits, for a short moment, all the travels she had with Hunter.

'It brings such a smile to my face, and I feel like saying thanks for taking me back there.'

Getting There

I was mooching about the buffet section of the Perth Qantas club, casually grazing over the options. I can usually make do with a drink and a small bowl of wasabi peas but on this afternoon I came across an epic dish.

Black bean Mexican salsa paste. It looked like it hadn't quite worked out but it was proving incredibly popular.

Why on earth a transit lounge would think that it's a good idea to feed customers such a potent mixture before they travel in a confined space across the continent is anyone's guess. It ensured there was more turbulence inside the plane than outside.

There was another little plaque beside the Mexican black bean paste that gave it a more attractive title: Comfort Food.

People will eat almost anything under that title. Call Brussels sprouts and broccoli a comfort food and they'll eat them. I happen to be a fervent admirer of both the broc and the sprout but there are some people who turn their noses up at tangling with members of the Brassicaceae family. (That's not some bad TV show name for a Mafioso clan, just what smart people call broccoli and Brussels sprouts.)

If you call something comfort food, there's a good chance it will be wolfed down by travellers and holiday-makers trying their best to find some respite from the business of getting where they are going.

Flying, in particular, is a method of transport that can be trying and requires that people use whatever gets them through the journey.

On a flight down to Melaleuca from Hobart on a small plane in rough weather, there was a woman who seemed to be incredibly and almost inexplicably calm. The pilot said that there might be a slight chance of having to abort the trip and return to Hobart because the flight necessitated a visual landing; 'If I don't see, we don't land.'

The weather was quite ordinary but it was the turbulence, the dipping and weaving, that was so startling and yet this particular woman was still serene.

After we had managed to land, thanks to the skill of the pilot and a break in the clouds that made the incredibly small landing strip visible, I asked her if she was a frequent visitor to this part of the world or was used to travelling in a light plane.

She smiled and said no, that in fact she was a fairly awful flyer but had learned a method that helped her cope.

'I got so nervous when I was flying to New Zealand for a holiday that I started eating something I liked, you know, just to make me feel better and take my mind off it all. Good old-fashioned comfort food. It got me through and now I make sure I have containers of it with me if I have to fly.'

I asked her what food it was that had given her such comfort.

She smiled again and searched through a backpack and showed me a plastic container of something.

'What is it?' I asked.

'Boiled onions, brandy and cream. And a few peppercorns for taste.'

A dangerous person to sit next to and one full of a concoction that would give the Mexican black bean salsa paste a run for its money.

When I was waiting to fly back out in the morning we all gathered by the little landing strip and heard the plane approaching. But we didn't see it and it didn't see us, so the plane flew back to Hobart.

In the afternoon the weather had cleared and so we waited again at the airstrip.

This time we saw and heard the plane. It landed and passengers emerged. Two were heading off to walk the wilderness tracks but were so discombobulated by the travelling experience they headed the wrong way and had to be pointed in the right direction.

Another passenger got off holding a plastic bag full of the contents of her stomach. Amazingly, she recognised me and asked if I could sign a book for her.

'Of course,' I said.

'Oh, thanks,' she said. 'Would you mind holding this?'

And as she bent down to rustle through her backpack I held her plastic bag and the recent stomach contents.

'Sorry,' she said. 'That trip was a shocker. This morning was bad when we had to turn back. But this one just about did me in.'

She laughed.

'Did you know there was a young American man on board this morning who told us he's flown all over the world but never had an experience like that flight. He was supposed to meet up with some friends tomorrow and then they'd walk back on the tracks together but he's decided to start out from Hobart and meet them halfway rather than get back in that bloody thing!'

I asked her if she had any comfort food to get her through the trip or to calm her down.

She eyed me and then took back her bag. 'If I had it didn't work because you've just been holding it!'

•

My brother is a renaissance man when it comes to holiday comfort food. He has a range of comfort foods, but I'll never forget him entering the kitchen after a frenetic day of flying and driving to a holiday on the Central Coast of New South Wales.

He bowled in and declaimed, 'What a bloody day.'

From the fridge and cupboards he then proceeded to create something that would make him feel better. White bread, the contents of a pickle jar – I think it was a piece of cauliflower (also of the Brassicaceae clan), a gherkin and some serrated carrots – tomato sauce, a slice of cheese, a small packet of Chicken Twisties and some frozen peas.

He ate this sandwich, which looked like the aftermath of the Battle of Culloden hamburger, took a deep sigh and closed his eyes and said warmly, 'Better.'

I try to keep up. In need of a bit of comfort after a trip home from a holiday that consisted of a series of connecting flights organised like a Chinese puzzle, I made Spam burgers. I accompanied them with a platoon of steamed dim sims and a longneck of Carbine stout.

Well, saying the dim sims were steamed makes them sound too healthy. I microwaved them. But there you have it, comfort.

Comfort food doesn't have to be eclectically unhealthy, I'm sure there are people who get a warm feeling by chowing down on handfuls of wheat germ or bran flakes.

As a rule of thumb, though, I think that the whole idea of comfort food is that it must be slightly naughty. Something you don't actually eat every day and know is an indulgence.

Spam burgers as an indulgence? Well, you never know what will make you comfortable and calm you down after getting where you have to go, or back from where you may have been on holiday.

Ice-cream is usually a staple, along with chocolate and biscuits.

Biscuits! A whole subculture of comfort unto themselves. Wagon Wheels, Anzacs, Mint Slice, Chocolate Royals.

Even Digestives and a glass of milk can do it for you if you're in the right mood.

There are many who'll put up their hands for anything that's fried. From fondue to the humble egg. That's what gives them a bit of digestive solace. And it's fun, nothing to be taken too seriously as long as you keep them as a therapeutic treat. Although the next time I'm flying from Perth, I'm not touching the black bean. Why? Just ask the guy who sat next to me.

•

The problem with flying is that there really isn't much you can do to control the situation.

You sit, strapped into a seat, at the mercy of whoever is playing on the in-flight entertainment system and the cabin crew.

The pilot is in charge of getting you where you might be headed and is mostly unseen. In fact, the only evidence of the existence of the pilot is a few bored words about where we are headed, the temperature there, and if we are lucky, a few descriptive phrases of what we might be able to see out our window down below.

The whole feeling of unease with flying begins with the basic idea that underpins any flight — that objects as heavy as airplanes shouldn't fly. But what makes things worse is that sometimes airlines try to jazz up the in-flight safety demonstration. I don't mind a straightforward relaying of familiar information. But startling people with in-flight safety demonstrations by trying to make them more entertaining never works.

I'm not the best of flyers but one time I was alarmed before the plane had even left the ground.

It was the beginning of the safety demonstration that did it. The Qantas introduction used to feature John Travolta in his ceremonial Qantas uniform.

It's a global world now but maybe having a Hollywood movie star, even one as pleasant as Mr Travolta, speaking in American tones about flying on an iconic Australian airline struck people as a bit odd.

Once I sat next to a woman who grumpily turned off her phone and said rather unkindly as Mr *Saturday Night Fever* drawled on, 'Why do we have a Scientologist? Do we get a free personality test to fill out on the sick bag to go with him?'

Well, it was a little unkind, but she was in the middle of a very important text.

Then John was given the elbow and replaced by two real-life Qantas pilots, both middle-aged men – presumably that's going to make you feel safer.

I'm a middle-aged man and know what dills we can be but nonetheless they both looked competent. One had the manner of a Maths teacher, advising us in curt tones to pay attention, sit back and enjoy the service. He might add, 'And finish the logarithms set and don't talk to the person sitting next to you.'

I could live with a Maths teacher flying – they deal in facts. It was the other middle-aged fellow in the uniform who worried me. He sounded like he was doing a Tony Abbott impersonation, but it wasn't the uber fit, hard-eyed man of action but a smiley, blissed-out yoga Tony version.

Unnerving.

Not because the prime minister isn't an effective politician. Despite his tendency to have photo opportunities in fluoro vests, safety goggles and hard hat draped over his politician's suit – to the point that one could mistake him for a well-dressed Village People tribute artist – he is an effective politician; you don't get to be prime minister for nothing. True, you may do nothing while you *are* prime minister, but that's another argument.

I wasn't sure about this whimsical, blissed-out yoga Tony being at the plane's controls.

It made me think of other incongruous pilots.

The pilot in the disaster movie *Airport*, who has to wrestle a stricken plane to safety. To my parents' amusement it was Dean Martin. Even though my parents loved Dino, this was a stretch.

'As if you'd get on with that coot flying the thing,' said Dad.

'Well, the announcements would be fun,' said my mum, 'and you'd be sure to get more than one drink too.'

'True.'

It was worse in the sequel, *Airport 1975*. After losing the pilots, an air hostess – they were called that back then – who was violently cross-eyed had to fly the plane before Charlton Heston and his hairpiece arrived to save the day.

The sequel to the sequel was creatively titled *Airport '77* and had a 747 airliner fall into the sea and begin to sink in the Bermuda Triangle.

Still, that was better than one other Qantas in-flight movie where a drug-addicted pilot miraculously managed to save most of the passengers on board a plane he spectacularly crashed, collecting a church steeple on the way down.

The man next to me was watching it as he worked his way through a cheese platter and Diet Coke. He looked across at me as I flicked my eyes at his screen, gave me the thumbs up and gleefully told me, 'It's a cracker, mate – hope he's flying the plane!'

It helps, of course, if whoever is flying the machine knows what he or she is doing. Even though I once had the pleasure of being flown by one of the best bush pilots in Australia from Dubbo to Sydney in a light plane, it rivalled the Melaleuca flight for sheer discomfort.

The night before we, the pilot included, were having a fine old barbecue get-together around the small lodge we were staying at in western New South Wales.

The pilot, it seemed, was having almost too good a time. He had an electric guitar and small portable amplifier.

He would strum the guitar, look at me and say, 'You'll probably be able to remember this one!' And he would play some indistinguishable jangling chords, a little like a kid who pretends to be able to play music.

I frowned, trying to pick the tune that I should probably have known.

He finished and said, 'Well?'

I shook my head.

'Oh God, "Brown-eyed Girl" by Van Morrison. Well, here's one you should know!'

And he repeated the process.

It was the same-sounding tinny jangle. He nodded his head up and down. I frowned.

He finished. 'Well?'

I thought I should say something, so I had a guess at 'Smoke on the Water'.

He stared back at me. 'Are you joking?'

I assured him I wasn't.

'Jesus, it's "Twist and Shout". Look, here's one you should know,' and he fired up again.

This, I think, went on for hours. The more I had to drink the worse it seemed my ear was. I never got close.

And each time he said, 'Well?', he seemed to get more irritated. The worst was when I thought he was playing 'Waterloo' by ABBA.

'Holy Moses! It's "Rock around the Clock"!'

We both stopped in the early hours of the morning and the next time I saw him he was methodically checking out his plane on the bush track.

There was another passenger who had flown with him before, and who had also been present at the songfest.

He pulled me aside and kindly reassured me. 'Look, he's one of the best pilots in Australia but he does like to have his bit of fun. I wouldn't worry if I was you, but I think it might be a bit rough to Sydney. Weather is closing in.'

I was given the front seat next to the lead guitarist and also a safety demonstration that made me long for blissed-out Tony.

The lead guitarist, who I think was a generous user of hair dye products, said, 'Righty-oh, Tin Ear Willy, strap yourself in nice and tight and hold on to that little Jesus handle if you think it'll do any good. This is going to bounce around like a right shitter.'

'You mean it's going to be stormy?'

'A bit. Don't worry, we've got some music we can listen to, help you settle the nerves. Bit of Patsy Cline, Buddy Holly, maybe even a bit of the old Big Bopper.'

All singers who had died in air crashes.

'You're having a lend, just trying to wind me up.'

He nodded. 'Too right. Music wouldn't do much good for you anyway, you wouldn't recognise a note.'

'Look,' I said, 'is this going to be rough?'

'Yes, mate, it will be a bit bouncy and there'll be a whiteout but we'll be right. You hang on, and if it helps you can listen to your iPhone.'

'Can I use it?'

'It won't interrupt anything but you won't hear much, I'm afraid. You'll be right.'

The lead guitarist was right: it did bounce around like a real shitter. But the most unnerving thing was the whiteout caused by the thick clouds. You couldn't see anything and the sense of not travelling was oddly disconcerting.

I tried to listen to some Dean Martin and that sort of soothed me but then I'm afraid I managed to think my way into a rather terrified state. I thought I should tell the people I loved that I loved them. It didn't make any difference that I was safe, I thought it would make them feel good to let them know that I loved them.

So I texted my son that I loved him.

I was texting my daughter when my son texted back.

'Have I done something?'

I replied, 'No.'

I thought and texted him, 'I want you to know I love you.'

He texted back. 'Ok. Where r you?'

I had called him and his sister the night before, about an hour before the weird guitarist and I began playing 'Name that Tune' so unsuccessfully, and let him know I was coming home from my break the next day.

But in my moment of panic, and as the little plane dipped a bit too much for my liking and all around was white, I texted back, 'I am in a small plane in a storm and am listening to Dean Martin. I am shitting myself.'

He texted back. 'Ha ha, Dino will get u through dad. Just keep the faith!'

I texted back 'Thanks'.

He texted back, 'But not like Tommy Lee Jones in *Under Siege.*' It is a film that we have seen on many a night down by the beach when we couldn't think of anything else to do. It was one of the first purchases we made from the local op shop.

A ridiculous film about terrorists, led by scenery-chewing Tommy Lee Jones and Gary Busey, taking over the battleship USS *Missouri* and being foiled by a strangely effective cook who used to be a Navy Seal. He is played by Steven Seagal with fake hair, fake tan, a girdle and about as much animation as a house brick, save for a perpetual look on his face as if he has just been offered a week-old egg sandwich for lunch.

It is very entertaining in a hokey, blokey nonsensical way.

In the end, Tommy Lee Jones has his face rearranged by fake tan Steven and then he's ploughed through some glowing screen in a control room somewhere. 'Keep the faith, Stranix!' is the merry send-off from fake-tan Steven.

I started smiling and then receive another text: 'Dino is best bet – you don't want to end up like tommy with a screwdriver in your head and shoved into navigational equipment.'

I laughed.

I texted him, 'What are you up to?'

He replied. 'Helping clean nanna's garden.'

Then again shortly after, 'Count yourself lucky in the storm. Nanna's on war path over her driveway plantings.'

Then another text. 'Love you Dad.'

Then another one, from my daughter. 'Clem told me to tell you I love you. I do. And to listen to Dean Martin. So listen x.'

Now I was laughing, and the lead guitarist tapped me on the shoulder and said through the intercom, 'You must be listening to some good music!'

I looked at my children's texts and gave the lead guitarist pilot the thumbs up. It's the best music.

And amazingly the flight didn't seem too bad after all as we floated down to earth and I caught a connecting flight home.

•

There was a time when people would get dressed up for air travel. Like my aunty Rita; she was flying back to the United Kingdom to visit her and my mother's relatives in Wales.

She parked her car at the side of our house and dropped off her ludicrously stupid dog Bruno for safekeeping in our backyard.

She was wearing a pantsuit outfit. A nifty ensemble that she usually wore only to socials at the Deception Bay Bowls Club and nights at the theatre or trips to 'do's' at the Redcliffe RSL. She also wore a bit of jewellery and put lipstick on as she got into our car to be driven to the airport.

'Don't know who I'll be sitting next to! So I have to make an effort to look a part of the jet set!'

Jet set – such a term of holidays past, hinting at life in the glamorous world of the jet travellers and holiday-makers of the 'jet age'.

That was a favourite phrase of my father's for a while, meant to signify that something was up to date and at the forefront of fashion and technology. Dad had never truly come to grips with my attempted high school perm and would always warn me as I trod off for a haircut, 'Just something sensible, cabbage head – no jet-age hairstyles for you.'

And Aunty Rita went off with a wave to spend another three hours at the terminal, even before she got on the plane.

These days anything is the go.

I have travelled in pyjamas on some long-haul holiday flights and on one flight saw an entire family wearing swimming costumes. Perhaps they were just saving time at the other end.

A nephew flying in for a holiday with us from his job as a mining engineer outdid this effort. He travelled with a wallet, a phone, a plastic bag full of three pairs of underpants and a toothbrush.

When one of my nieces returned from Thailand, from her 'Schoolies' trip, she wore a pair of sandals and a sarong.

Schoolies is a holiday week of celebrations that most final-year students consider a rite of passage. What began as an impromptu gathering of high school graduates at the Broadbeach hotel on the Gold Coast in the early eighties has ended up a multi-million-dollar economic bonanza.

There have been all sorts of subcultures born. 'Toolies' are over-age participants who want to hang around and join in the fun, and 'Droolies' are worse, hangers-on who, in the words of some of my son's friends, are on the prowl for some 'young flesh'.

My son went to Byron Bay and said that it wasn't too bad a week. 'It was a bit of fun but it really wasn't all that it was cracked up to be,' he later told me.

At least, he said, he didn't get hit like a couple of his mates. A big lad, he said he was hard to miss and made an easy target for locals who didn't like the idea of 'up-themselves out-of-town schoolies' parading around the local haunts. But he'd managed not to get into any trouble.

I asked him who hit his friends.

He shrugged his big shoulders. 'Don't know, didn't see them. But we think they were Ragies.'

Ragies, it seems, are local lads, supposedly tradies who are full of beer and bad manners and take a swing when the mood strikes them at the offending Schoolie participant.

The resulting attacks have all sorts of terms: king hits, cheap shots, coward punches, ambushes or mob shots.

It's like a demographic, socio-economic hamburger with the lot.

It sounds awful and if you don't participate, it probably is. Every year the whole Schoolies festival provides fodder for sensational news stories of drunken behaviour, drink-spiking and misadventure.

It's reached the point where some parents even tag along just to keep an eye on their offspring.

It's also grown international. In Perth, Schoolies can pop over to Bali and in the eastern states cheaper airfares opened up places like Thailand for the week of celebration.

It's become a self-perpetuating industry event, and all elements of the Schoolies season, from finger-wagging shock jocks and disapproving tabloids with headlines that glory in the gossip and sanctimonious tut-tutting, to the tourist businesses and government revenue departments that salivate at the thought of teenage coin, actively encourage the whole event.

It seemed appropriate that I caught a flight with a brigade of wasted and fatigued teenagers returning from all points of the known Schoolies compass.

I looked around at them, these holiday travellers returning from living through what a friend of mine, who is a teacher, calls confected rites of passage. Some were very sunburned, some looked incredibly young, some disappointed and some shredded.

A girl was very sick into the first thing she could grab a hold of, which was her friend's bag. They laughed a little, and the stewards were nice and considerate. They even cut some slack to a loud boy who obviously had tickets on himself after a good week away.

And then my old friend popped up on the screen. Time for the in-flight safety demonstration.

This time there was an excruciating Olympic theme, which featured sports people dressed in their tracksuits speaking into the camera about teamwork and paying attention to exits and seat belts.

Someone in marketing obviously thought this sporting approach worked well because the supposed national carrier went on to feature Australian cricketers in the safety demo. Blissed-out Tony still featured as emcee, as well as a steward who smiled as if demonstrating a grimace that might feature in the centrefold of *Orthodontists' Monthly*. Then, marching through the aisle dressed in baggy greens and blazer, came Michael Clarke and a clutch of cricketers.

As cricketers these men are very good. I used to think Michael Clarke was a bit flaky, not because of his inky tatts but because he had a tendency to get out on the last ball of a session, or in fact the final ball of the day.

Well, Michael, I was proved wrong by a glorious run with the bat, a personally charming manner and a willing and enthusiastic approach to the game so many of us love. Ricky Ponting is a champion beyond words and Peter Siddle and Mathew Wade have talent to spare.

But in a safety demonstration?

I have an ability to look completely ridiculous when I act. 'So wooden that you could build a house extension out of him,' one critic kindly wrote of an acting effort. I hate to say this, but these wearers of the baggy green looked about as natural and as comfortable as one of those appalling videos of captives performing for a band of extremists.

The fascination with sporting themes probably means come winter we'll have rugby players kitted out in their playing gear and mouthguards, fastening seatbelts and pointing with dislocated fingers to the nearest exit.

The setting of the brace position could at least give the forwards some extra practice in setting a scrum. A nice touch could be an overly officious steward-cum-referee crying out, 'Crouch, touch, engage!'

Then they could blow a whistle and reset and reset.

But why stop at sportspeople aiding blissed-out Tony in the safety demo?

There are so many others who could help officiate the ceremony of the safety demonstration.

There is the harried family off on holiday with an odd assortment of baggage and children to wrangle as life vests, lights and whistles are pointed to and draped around a head.

Or the grumpy businessperson who is too busy texting, or checking a furtive tablet in a last-minute attempt to scrape more connection to whatever it is that is so important for them, to pay any attention to the demonstration.

Or maybe a clutch of kids returning from Schoolies. A little uncertain, unsure of where they may be heading and wondering about the worth of the certainties that they are leaving behind.

The flight went up and it landed safely enough and we shuffled down the aisle like manacled convicts and then off and into the terminal.

Some of the kids were embraced by parents.

The girl who had been sick into her friend's bag smiled warmly and was gracious as she kissed both her parents. She laughed lightly and said that she had had a really great time but was glad to be home.

The boy who had been a bit too loud and was intent on being the star on the plane burst into tears when his parents hugged him.

At the end of the holidays celebrating the end of their schooling, the different reactions from different kids made me wonder just what their week had been like.

Some parents smiled like blissed-out Tony with that wide vacant grin, wondering just what their child had gone through on that first post-school holiday.

I walked on and then I saw him.

Yes, it was him. I was sure. Just in front of me, marching along determinedly with a coterie of people following in step. A few heads turned as he moved through the terminal. The girl who had been sick into her friend's bag, and whose manner now was like butter wouldn't melt in her mouth, watched him and pointed to her mother to turn around and take a look.

It was Tony Abbott. The real one.

I laughed like a drain.

Doing Nothing

I asked Nick where he was pedalling to on his accrued holidays this year. He's a mad lycra wearer and even madder cyclist who has ridden just about everywhere you can in Australia.

'Nowhere.' He shook his head. 'Not this break.'

'You're joking,' I said.

'No, I'm not.' He shook his fit head that sat on top of his fit body. 'No. I am not kidding. I'll just hang around the place and kick back, do nothing.'

I remembered about six years ago when he planned to spend his three-week holiday painting his house.

The first two weeks he was always happily in overalls and with a transistor radio, little scrapers, the occasional sander and tubes of gap filler.

He said he was having a ball. And he looked like he was, a retro picture of do-it-yourself happiness.

Then in the third week something happened. It rained a couple of nights and the thought must have struck him that he wasn't going to finish.

Then there was no happy chatting as he sat on a plank between two painter's trestles, no friendly waving and nods of the head as he prepared his paint, spray machine and brushes.

Just mad frenetic activity, like a sped-up Jerry Lewis movie. And lots of pained yelling and frustrated swearing.

His do-it-yourself house painting turned in to a do-it-yourself mental breakdown.

How he got it done was amazing but he returned to work, in his wife's words, 'Absolutely buggered, in the mind and body. I told him he was never to do it again.'

I looked at him now, smiling at me at this pleasant neighbourhood barbecue.

'House needs another coat?' I asked him.

'Oh, up yours, smartarse. Look, that counts as doing nothing. Technically, working around your home, doing it up, counts as doing nothing.'

'How do you mean?'

'Well, you don't leave your suburb, you don't fly, you've got nothing to really see or do. Just hang around and do nothing.'

This, I thought, made some sort of sense. He thought for a minute and then said slowly, 'Of course, you may end up in therapy but, still, it counts as doing nothing.'

Then he laughed a little, 'Jesus, I needed stress leave after that holiday.'

Another man at the barbecue, who was handing a bowl of chips around, offered his thoughts.

'Well, you'll be watching the tour, Nick, won't you?'

'Yes, I dare say I'll be tuning in.'

The man with the chips was an avid bike rider as well and every July would hold spinning tour parties at his house. This consisted of inviting a few friends around to his shed, which had a big television mounted on the wall and a series of bike mounts, where you could wear your favourite team's lycra and pedal your bike as fast as you liked without going anywhere as you watched the skinny Tour de France riders race around the scenery on their bikes.

It really was weirder than the Masons and I, frankly, thought the man with the bowl of chips quite mad. I suspected he probably slept in his lycra riding outfit.

He turned to me and said, 'I can't believe you don't watch the tour, William.'

I can believe I don't watch the tour.

'But it's just enthralling,' said another man who was a teacher.

'How do you mean?' I asked. I also thought it quite amazing that somebody would actually use the word enthralling at a barbecue. Good on them.

'The politics and the tactics, just enthralling.'

Already the overuse of enthralling had crossed the line of a friendly get-together.

'And the scenery,' added a lovely man who was not only an avid cyclist but another neighbour and an all-round good egg.

I shrugged. Then another guest, a doctor who volunteers his services to overseas aid organisations, joined in with a tone that should only be used at barbecues when somebody has pinched your chop.

'You don't like the tour, don't like cycling, do you?'

I admitted I didn't.

'But you played a lot of rugby, didn't you?'

I admitted I did.

'I've seen the way you walk – "high-impact hobble", I like to call it,' said the volunteering doctor. 'And I bet you'll watch rugby and league and all the other sports.'

I admitted I did.

'There are drugs in other sports.'

I never mentioned drugs.

'You don't like the tour? But what about the scenery?'

The scenery? Well, go watch *The Sound of Music*. Lots of green valleys and mountains there; no lycra, to be sure, but lots of scenery.

I have no doubt about the stamina and endurance it takes to engage in the sporting endeavour of pushing your feet around a set of pedals. I think people such as Cadel Evans, Mark Cavendish and Bradley Wiggins and their like are amazing athletes.

I just don't like the tour or road cycling.

This is what the nice people – and they were nice people – at the barbie didn't get. They looked on in a mixture of pity and disbelief, like most cultists who come across an unbeliever. Sadly, I've always been in that bracket.

Blame it perhaps on me falling off my pushbike when I attempted to stand on the seat going down the King Street hill one day when I was coming home from school. On the last day before the holiday break. I thought I was celebrating. So was the kid who had loosened the front wheel at lunchtime.

Whatever my dubious history with bicycles and my inclination to not partake with my middle-aged brothers in squeezing into clingy quarter-onesies, I could definitely say that skinny guys in lycra and advertising slogans don't do it for me.

Especially on holidays.

And as a small kid the whole bike thing just seemed none too sensible. This was proved by watching the special event segments on *Sportscene* on Channel Seven in the seventies. After the pass the football competition, there was the rowing machine competition – we all cheered my brother's friend Zoom when he was on and got done by some bloke from Churchie – and then the weight-lifting with a large friendly man who had a restaurant not far from Lang Park. Then there was the woodchopping, with enormous people balancing on what looked like pieces of playground equipment.

Gigantic people with flailing axes and lots of chips of wood flying everywhere. I liked that.

Then there was the cycling, two people in tight outfits and big helmets on a fixed bike in a TV studio at the top of

Mt Coot-tha. They looked, well, odd. We all laughed when the host, Rod Gallegos, said, 'Pedal faster, son — the lights are getting brighter.'

I'm sure it's a great sport. Just not my thing.

Perhaps if there were some contestants on the tour pedalling up and down and through the scenery on a Malvern Star Dragster, complete with streamers pouring from the ape hanger handlebars, and with whitewall tyres, that might tempt me. And it certainly doesn't come under my understanding of doing nothing on your holidays. It's simply too energetic, too focused, to be 'doing nothing'.

Pedalling slowly around on a bike counts as doing nothing. Like me and my mother having lunch and enjoying it way too much when she came and holidayed with my family down in Melbourne. She decided that riding a tandem bicycle along the Yarra River and surrounds at peak hour and singing songs from some of her favourite musicals, like *The Desert Song* and *Carousel*, was what we should do on holiday.

It was a minor miracle that we didn't end up at the bottom of the Yarra at the end of the second chorus of 'You'll Never Walk Alone' or under a tram to the tune of 'My Desert is Waiting'.

But that is the cycling definition of doing nothing on holidays.

•

Doing nothing can happen quite a lot when you're on holidays and most usually during holidays that are festive.

It may be Easter, after the Easter egg hunt is over and everyone is flopping down to engage in the ritualistic watching of bad Easter movies on television.

Never-ending Jesus films as long as a test match. *The Robe* got a good going over. Mum liked Richard Burton. It was always slightly odd because the film was shot in a widescreen format so on the telly you only ever saw pots or pillars growling out in a Welsh accent.

'Oh, he's lovely. It's before the booze knocked him sideways. Look at him.'

Sometimes you'd see young Richard, looking rather fetching in Roman breastplate and permed hair, hamming away for all he was worth. Then just as suddenly his voice would be seemingly coming from a pillar or a bowl of fruit. Then fetching young Burton would reappear and sound campy like the nasty villainous emperor or syrupy and girly like Jean Simmons.

The film ratio didn't really work that well on our old Pye telly but it wouldn't make much difference, every Easter we'd tune in. Doing nothing demanded it.

Years later, down the beach at the Mornington Peninsula, we all sat around the TV on a rainy Easter Sunday.

The Robe was on.

'He's cute,' said one of my nieces, looking at a long-dead Richard Burton snarling away in his breastplate.

'My mum liked him,' I said as I sat eating the ear of a chocolate Easter bunny. 'Although I liked him when he looked like a bowl of fruit.'

'Too much chocolate for you, Uncle William,' said another of my nieces.

There were other Easter films that called around once a year like old friends to say hello. A crazy film called *Barabbas*. It's a film about one of the thieves that were released when Christ was condemned. It goes on forever and makes no sense and was memorable only for one of my father's sayings, which he used to cry at the rugby when someone got away with something.

'That bastard is as lucky as Barabbas!'

Ben-Hur, which was as camp as a row of tents, and the immortal uber Jesus film, *The Greatest Story Ever Told*. This was one of my favourites, with Max von Sydow as Christ. He walked around looking incredibly depressed about the whole business of being the Messiah. And really, who can blame him, the way things turned out? He barely raised a sweat in turning out the moneylenders from the temple and when Lazarus got up he looked as if he couldn't give two hoots about raising the dead.

The highlight, though, was John Wayne, straight from some Western saloon, portraying the Roman centurion at the bottom of the cross.

Squeezed into a Roman tunic, his great face crumpled into a prune under his helmet, he intones, 'Truly this man was the son-na GAWWWWD.'

We used to howl with laughter. Even Mum. Doing nothing never seemed so good.

•

Movies are a prime source of doing nothing on holidays because you go to see the most improbable films simply because they are holiday films.

There is that floating period in all Australian cities between Christmas Day and New Year when time expands and the temperature seems to soar.

It's forty degrees and everybody is trying to get over their Christmas gorging; it's cool and dark in the cinema so nobody really cares. You can tell that by the films people make. Usually they are unremitting tripe with no point at all. Trying to find one that a 'family' can enjoy is another thing. And what is a family movie?

On a hot day you are governed by the nearest session time and the lowest movie rating. That is what brought us to *Alien vs Predator – Requiem*. It caught my eye because it was listed under the banner of 'Goodtime, Summertime Movie Fun!'

'What's it about?' one of the kids in front of us had asked the teenage ticket collector. Without the slightest hint of irony, in a breaking voice, the teenager read out the synopsis.

'Two of the greatest demons in movie history face off in a unique and originally exciting battle to the death. MA15.' Summertime movie fun indeed.

•

There comes a time in a man's life when he knows he must move on, the moment of goodbye to an old friend, no matter how many good and bad times you've lived through.

And oddly enough it is born from two types of doing nothing on a holiday that are a rite of passage for many Australian fathers.

Haven't gone through it? Don't worry, sooner or later your time will come. It's the farewell to an old and trusted servant. A titan of the backyard – the trampoline. Yes, old Trampo.

It's a wonder of the backyard that arrives only on big occasions and remains an important piece of childhood infrastructure.

In the case of our oval trampoline, it arrived one long-ago Christmas in a large cardboard box which I wrapped up in the late hours of Christmas Eve. That feat was a wonder in itself – it took forever and at times seemed like I was wrapping up an oil rig – but the look on the kids' faces when they'd finished attacking the presents under the tree and were told there was something out the back for them rated pretty high on the scale of lovely wonder.

But the real magic was to come on Boxing Day. This is another seminal moment in a parent's life, when the present bought has to be put together and constructed.

Heavy rain had fallen almost continuously on Christmas Day and their mother had assured the kids that all would be sorted tomorrow. By me.

This posed a slight problem as I had very poor form with regards to putting things up by myself. Numerous barbecues, that were about as well put together as Collins-class subma-rines – they were just as leaky – and all those dream designs from IKEA that crumbled into dust under my guiding hand.

The other problem was that it was Boxing Day. A classic moment on the doing nothing calendar. Cricket. Australia and South Africa, so I was more manic than usual.

It takes a special effort to put something as big as a trampoline together yourself and, even after having the box collapse on top of me, which prompted a few magic words, somehow the components came together to become something metal and then something round and then it became a trampoline and soon it became Trampo.

It was a good Boxing Day. Matthew Hayden took an absolute screamer at gully and my kids hugged me and yelled in happy incredulity, 'You made this, Dad – and it WORKS!'

Over the years Trampo worked beautifully. It was part babysitter and part ballroom, a castle, a ship or whatever a kid's imagination wanted it to be.

True, there was always the element of danger and drama associated with imagined catastrophe that caused parents to yell warnings, but thankfully nothing really ever eventuated.

Although there were the mysterious holes that appeared, perfectly symmetrical, which my son assured me were the result of a school science experiment. I never asked what type of school experiment is conducted on a trampoline during the holidays. Best left as a bit of backyard folklore. The true glory of old Trampo was that wonderful feeling of leaving the earth, flying for a bit, waiting for your tummy to catch up and then plummeting back down all together.

Seeing little people double-bounce and try to disappear into the tree.

But kids grow up. Puff the Magic Dragon time.

There really isn't much more of an obvious target for the hard rubbish day than old Trampo.

I walked out, patted old Trampo. Almost as if it were a favourite horse that had gone lame. Looked at the tree house. The kids always wanted to jump from there onto Trampo. So I decided to say goodbye with a last bounce.

I climbed the tree, checked out where those school holiday science experiment holes were and noticed that they had grown considerably, but took a deep breath and jumped out into space. I jumped on Trampo and bounced off into the garden of rose bushes. And a forgotten statue. Much more usage of magic words. Much pain. Time to say goodbye.

•

Some of the best moments on holidays can be when you and those around you are engaged in doing nothing.

Like taking time out from tours and outings and just hanging out by the pool – a go-to doing-nothing pastime. And almost magically when you do nothing, you remember doing nothing pastimes from years before.

I bomb-dived and came up floating at the deep end with my kids in a swimming pool littered with a various array of swimming costumes and nationalities. The bomb dive was a competition the kids and I were having.

Then I remembered. I was about ten at a Saturday game at Lang Park between Redcliffe and Souths in which I wasn't very interested because Redcliffe was getting beaten, so my mother played a favourite game of looking at people in the crowd and making up stories about them.

'That man over there.' She pointed to a man with a long beard and regal bearing. 'That man is a Russian count.'

I looked at the guy. I didn't know that Russian counts wore Stubbies, thongs and a 4IP Colour Radio t-shirt.

The Russian count opened his mouth and gave a massive roar. 'Get us two Chiko rolls! Two of 'em! Will ya?'

He then scratched his vitals and picked his nose a bit.

'He's from Kippa-Ring,' my father said.

Who'd have thought that Russian counts from Kippa-Ring liked Chiko rolls? It was a fun game and made the Dolphins getting beaten seem like a manageable thing.

'Now that is a game,' my mother said, 'you can play when you're doing nothing and pretty soon you realise that doing nothing can be quite a lot of fun . . .'

Years later in that pool, in between bombs, I thought I'd play that game. A rotund old man in puke-yellow swimming trunks carefully lowered himself down the pool ladder. He was bald with wisps of white hair crowning his head.

'That man,' I said to my kids, 'that man looks like an English lord.'

My kids stared at me. Over at the old man. Back at me.

'He looks like an English lord?' said my son.

'Yeah,' I said. I told them about my mum's game.

'Why would an English lord wear swimmers like that?'

'English lords don't care what they look like,' I said.

Lord Yellow Puke stopped halfway down the ladder and said something very loudly in a language that could have come from *Star Trek*. European, I think – but you didn't need to understand to comprehend that the non-English lord was emitting the international cry of, 'Shivers, this water is cold!'

The kids soon got the hang of the game. A tanned man with red, white and blue board shorts, gold bracelet and gold crucifix around his neck was a holidaying gangster from New York. He was reading a book entitled *The Secrets of Corporate Business*.

A laughing woman and her partner were eloping newly-weds. My daughter decided she was the opera singer daughter of a wealthy Italian industrialist and he was a struggling young doctor who worked among the poor. He also played lead guitar in a rock band.

I asked what books my daughter had been reading lately. She laughed.

A mother playing catch with her son was a kung-fu master and a spy when she wasn't on holiday.

The little boy was a hired villager and she wasn't on holiday, she was spying on the English lord, who was still halfway down the ladder yelling to two vast people on straining poolside lounges.

My daughter wondered if we were subjects of similar speculation.

I shrugged, declaring, 'Going to chuck a Horsey Dive!'

Hauling my middle-aged body out of the pool I heard a bored British voice – I think it was the rock guitarist doctor boyfriend of the opera singer.

'See – I told you they were Australian.'

Not much mystery to us. And why would there be, we were on holidays, doing nothing.

Going Back

Standing around a cold park on a Melbourne Sunday winter's morning watching our cold daughters play lacrosse can be, oddly, a pleasant thing to do.

'Oh, that girl is so rough,' said the father of a tall girl who plays with my daughter.

'Oh yes, she's a shocker. And my Stephanie says you should see her getting on the train in the morning for school. Like a rugby scrum,' said Kath, the mother of Stephanie and three other girls who all played lacrosse.

Another woman pretended to smoke cigarettes with her husband, blowing out vast streams of frosty air from her mouth. 'Wanna drag?' she asked, and laughed.

He looked at her and said, 'Well, I'd be more impressed if you could blow smoke rings.'

His wife tried.

'Careful, you'll get arrested,' he said.

We all laughed. Then we all mimicked taking huge drags and blowing out the 'smoke'. Aping what we had probably all done at one time or another when we were kids on a cold winter's morning.

They're a nice bunch of people on the sporting parent acquaintances graph and it's a good game, lacrosse; girls running everywhere, going flat out, although it can get a bit rough and the rules can be a little hard to understand.

The girl who is like a rugby scrum getting on the train crashed into somebody.

'Isn't that illegal?' I asked.

'No, no, it was rough but not illegal,' said Kath and then she smiled and turned to me. 'All the years you've been watching it and you don't know the rules.'

I admit I could have tried harder but it is such a quick game and some of the decisions and rules befuddle me.

'Well, years and years it may be but, you know, some things just don't sink in.'

'Oh, come on, you – if you don't learn things then you'll be in trouble.'

The tall girl's father laughed. 'You going to leave a day late for the Murray again this year then, Kath?'

Kath is Irish and has a cracking accent and temperament to

go with it and, in between cheering on her girls and giving advice to the umpires, she laughs a lot.

'Oh no, never again – come on, umpire, illegal check! – I'm not losing that space again, I can tell you that for nothing.'

'What space?' I asked and then a player, who happened to be my daughter, shunted someone into the ground. 'Isn't that —' I half got out.

'Good girl!' yelled Kath.

'Isn't that illegal?' I finished.

'Oh, for goodness sake, not when it's your own daughter.' She laughed. 'Of course not, it was a good check.'

I nodded, a bit confused and asked about the space again.

'Ah, the space!' The tall girl's father laughed.

'It's our camping spot on the Murray. We've been going for years and then last year I wanted to leave a day later and, because of that, these people took it. I could have scratched my eyes out.'

'Your spot?'

'Yes, our spot, our camping spot by the Murray River.'

'It is a public camping ground, Kath, so technically it can be anybody's,' said the tall girl's father.

Kath laughed. 'Well, that's the rumour but we've been using that spot for years.'

'What did you do?' I asked.

'Oh, we got the spot next to it.' She roared with laughter again. 'It wasn't that bad and the people were nice, but it was just our spot – never again.'

Camping. In the same spot. For years. I shivered a little.

Not just because of the weather but also at the thought of camping.

My wife Sarah Watt once described me as being the King of Ponces because I said at a dinner party that my idea of camping was a hotel room with no mini bar and no Foxtel.

I freely admit I am a ponce but it was, in my defence, an attempt at humour.

Camping is a mystery to me and doing it in the same place year after year is an even bigger riddle.

'So you've been going to the same place for how long?'

'Oh, since the second one was born . . . say, twenty-three years. It's been marvellous.'

'What do you like about it?'

'Camping?' she said, as if she couldn't quite believe that anybody would ask this in the tone that I'd used.

I nodded.

'Well, everything. The family being together, the air, the people you get to know and see that time of the year. The little get-togethers you have. The campfires you build. The kids growing up.'

'And you go to the same place?'

'Well, yes. It might be boring to some folk, but when you're on a good thing why not stick to it?' She smiled and was going to say something else and then she screamed in delight. 'Oh, good goal, Steph! Good goal!'

I applauded along with the other parents and then we all tried to blow smoke rings with our breath on the cold winter's air.

The idea of going back to one particular place for holidays is one that people have more often than you think.

Kath and her family and all the other people who went back to that same camping spot on the Murray weren't alone. The former Prime Minister John Howard and his family went to the same coastal town of Hawks Nest each year for over two decades for their holidays.

There Mr Howard would wait in line with others at the local bakery and do his early morning walks along the beach, what some other holiday-makers would refer to as his 'lap of honour'.

So if it was good enough for one of the country's most successful prime ministers, then why shouldn't we all do it?

Perhaps it's the repetition of the routine that makes it soothing and relaxing; you know what you're going to get and, as Kath said, 'When you're on a good thing, stick to it.'

For nearly all of us, sooner or later a holiday will take us back to a place we have been before.

And sometimes you can see it in a whole new way.

•

'Hey,' said my friend as we walked through the city on our way to Brisbane's West End. 'Let's take one of these bikes.'

'Okay,' I said.

The little blue bikes seemed friendly. A bank of cycles that dotted the CBD. I managed to finally make the machine that lets you hire the bike, hire them to me. Then I had difficulty unhooking the friendly bike. Finally, after looking like I was trying to break something, the bike popped off. The bikes looked like they would fit Campbell Newman. They were premier-sized.

I am not. Say what you want about Campbell Newman, he is a lot fitter than me.

I saw myself reflected in a window.

A prime piece of aged beef. Imperial measurements of six foot four and fifteen and a half stone. People laughed as the bike disappeared beneath me.

It reminded me of a video I was shown on the internet of a circus bear riding a bike. People were outraged about that. Even though I looked like a podgy bear in Bermuda shorts, nobody was outraged, just amused.

Riding to West End I discovered a hill in Vulture Street I never knew existed. I started sweating. On my little bike, with my big legs and bad knees and circus-bear riding style, I looked like a mobile sprinkler as I sprayed sweat.

The bike helmet squashed my panama ponce top hat and I suddenly wondered what people in this city did before air conditioning.

Then I remembered. I grew up in a house without air conditioning. Lots of people did. You opened windows. Waited for the change to come. Before that, you stood under the hose. Wandered to the beach. Or, if you couldn't be bothered, you'd jump into an above-ground pool and then slide around the sides until the chlorinated water created a whirlpool that carried you around and around like the washing on a slow cycle.

I chugged along and thought, what a glorious floating feeling that was, just staring up at the sky and gently spinning.

I don't suppose many people have above-ground pools anymore. Perhaps it's a good thing. I can remember the yelling of countless parents: 'Don't double up on the chlorine tablets! You'll end up like a pickled bloody onion.'

I felt like laughing when I remembered a friend's mother using the pool to wash some clothes when the water mains were cut. She told us to 'Kick your legs faster, beat the water like a shark's about to get you. Faster!'

I felt a pang of something and I'm not sure what. Perhaps it was in my knees as I tried to ride a bit faster. There's no way now I could churn the water in an above-ground pool like a washing machine now.

And those clothes, I thought, they were business shirts, and undies – they must have stunk of chorine and itched like anything. But my friend's mum was happy.

•

It's when the memories of a place, and the people who passed the time there with you, all come colliding with the present that the acute feeling of simply being a human can be so great.

On holidays in Western Australia, walking up a hill, I stopped and thought, of all things, of the funeral of my brother-in-law, when I sat in a church filled with people who were there to pay their respects, to try to find solace for themselves and give support to his family in a communal expression of grief and love. To perhaps make some sense of how a man so loved and liked could die so young.

There came a moment after the eulogy and speeches and songs when everyone in the church sat still and a slide show played on a screen before us.

'A reflection,' said the priest.

The images were from my brother-in-law's life, of him and his family and then his girlfriend, who became his wife.

And then the family they had made. We all stared; at times it was too hard and around the church there were tears. But then a dawning. These images were so joyous and so rich. Groans of recognition and laughter.

My wife giggled and said to her sister, 'Do you remember that bloody holiday?'

My sister-in-law laughed.

'How could I forget?'

It was spectacular, where one by one all of us had fallen ill with what our host, universally known as Grandmother, called rather unreconstructively, 'a bloody awful wog with more runs than Bradman'.

'And all before lunch too!' a helpful son-in-law had offered.

A holiday. So many images upon the screen were of holidays.

It was as if a life, and a good one like my brother-in-law's, could have its happiness measured in them.

All this I thought when I was standing on the hill looking out at the Great Southern Ocean in Albany.

I had a cold and so had made my way through the town to the chemist for potions. Albany is a pretty place. Historic buildings, an unchanged town centre, and views to the southern ocean.

I passed a statue of an Indigenous man called Mokare, who had helped the early Europeans navigate the area and tried to broker better relations between the different groups.

Sometime back the statue was painted white, somebody making their point that perhaps Mokare's help and advice wasn't welcome.

Shame, it's a fine statue and Mokare seemed a remarkable man.

Not far from Mokare, a couple of Falun Gong practitioners were Falun Gonging it up in a park. A banner attempted to explain Falun Gong but the writing was too small. Was it religious, martial arts or political? I looked but was no wiser.

Across the road two Jehovah's Witnesses plied their trade with a stand of literature.

Further down, a middle-aged busker played saxophone energetically with taped backing music. She'd built up quite a sweat, hopping about playing a tune. I recognised it, but the title escaped me.

I remembered it was also known as a ditty, 'Hitler Has Only Got One Ball'. There was an old man with a walking frame nearby so I asked what the tune's proper name was. He thought and after an age said, 'Hitler Has Only Got One Ball'.

I nodded.

The Jehovah's Witnesses and the Falun Gongs and the busker played on.

Across the water, high on a ridge, a platoon of tall wind turbines sprouted. Against the history of the place they seemed a modern intrusion. This town made me think of Redcliffe and Moreton Bay, on the other side of the continent.

Like Redcliffe, Albany was the site of its state's first European settlement and both were forsaken as the capital for another place by a river.

But unlike Redcliffe, the sparseness of Western Australia and the distance from the growing capital ensure Albany is cocooned. Walk through the town and the past echoes with each step. Just like the busker's saxophone. There's something slightly mad but also reassuring about listening to 'Tijuana Taxi' and looking down the main street of a town that reminds you of where you grew up.

As in Moreton Bay, whaling was once an industry in Albany. Whale watching is a thriving business on both sides of the country today, but it's startling to think that Australia's whaling industry ceased operations in 1978 in Albany. And that Tangalooma's whaling station in Moreton Bay closed in 1962.

Not that long ago in a nation's history.

I think of the last time I was on the islands of Moreton Bay.

It was North Stradbroke and I was walking on top of the cliffs not far from Main Beach. The kids were still asleep and I'd waddled off for an early morning walk.

The water on a fine day is beautiful. It has the white of the breaking waves, the clearness of the shallows that turns into the rolling turquoise of the outer waves where dolphins surf the surge, breaking through the surface.

And then out to the blue-black of the deep. My wife, Sarah Watt, loved it here, just at this point. We stood together with our children on the last holiday we had before she died.

She laughed. Laughed because she was so in love with that moment of life.

Then out to sea she could see the spouts of migrating whales. We all pointed, all in different directions.

She held my hand suddenly, and said softly, 'Hey, you up there.'

And I turned to her and she kissed me.

On that morning by myself I looked out to the sea. No dolphins surfing, but it was beautiful.

At moments like that when the presence of someone you have loved is close, a strange sort of numbness that holds pain and joy and love descends. There is not much that is dignified about death but there is a grace that can be attained.

How a person meets their death should not define their life, but in her final days there were moments that exemplified Sarah Watt's spirit.

Early one morning she called to me. 'I saw whales. Out there.' She pointed out through our front windows. 'Just look.'

Rubbish trucks were doing the weekly pick-up.

One drew near and stopped, its arm reaching out. If

you cradled your imagination, it looked like the flukes of a whale rolling.

The street streamed with golden light and the morning dew had fallen.

'There,' said Sarah, smiling, 'I told you.'

And somehow in that moment of whimsy and delight, suggesting an idea, she animated the street.

It was quite frankly magical.

'They're picking up rubbish,' I said.

'Don't we have clever whales in our street,' she said softly.

I remembered her saying that to me as she sat in the front room and as I stood out in the near deep at North Stradbroke a whale breached spectacularly. It threw itself almost from the water and turned in the early morning sun.

It was so joyous, an exaltation of life, that I let out a cry.

I kept staring and then a series of whales, almost as if directed, breached in synchrony.

I held my breath.

Then from down the walk a little way came a voice. 'Jeez, they're putting on a show!'

I looked at the man. I knew him slightly.

A tough-looking bloke who worked in the local bottle shop. He nodded to me as he came closer.

I stared out to where the whales had danced.

'How are you?' he said as he came closer.

I could barely say anything really, and then this man who looked as if he could pack down in any front row you could care to name stood not far from me and did something quite unexpected.

'You right?' he said.

I said I was and shrugged my shoulders.

Then he stepped towards me and said, 'I know who you're thinking of, matey. I'm sorry. Come here.'

And he gave me a bear hug.

I cried.

'It's a beautiful morning,' he said and he nodded. 'She would have loved it.'

Then he walked off.

I stood in Albany and remembered that lovely act of random kindness. The light and the sky were open and beautiful, and so many souls and people and places raced around within me. Before I was even thought of, my mother took my brother and sisters to Tangalooma's whaling station on a day trip, a hit and run holiday if you like, in its last days of operation. There is a photo of them standing with grimacing smiles on a jetty. My mother has a look of unbearable sadness on her face.

Below them the flensing took place. The separation of the blubber from the whale's flesh.

Mum had a romantic view of whalers gathered from sea tales like Melville's *Moby-Dick*. The reality, of course, is practically always a very different thing.

I looked around the pretty town and saw the picturesque old Albany jail, now a museum of sorts.

I thought of the people who had been confined within its cold walls. Close enough to hear the frolicking of the pubs.

I thought of all those souls who came and went in this town. How we all come and go.

How, if we are lucky and are loved enough, we might become cherished holiday memories, for holidays may be the realest, most sweetest part of life.

Overhead a sea bird sailed through the ocean's breeze. I heard so many voices and felt close to so many people.

The least I could do, I decided, was to buy a CD from the busker.

She looked a bit surprised. Well, it's something to remember Albany.

And after all, I'm on holiday.

Acknowledgements

I'd like to thank, in no particular order, Alison Telford, Sue Byrne, Rick McCosker, Peter Bolton, Deonie Fiford, Karen Ward, Anna Egelstaff, Bevan Bleakely, Clem and Stella McInnes, Leon Teague, Niall Mather. And Bernadette Foley – a wonderful publisher and an even better friend.

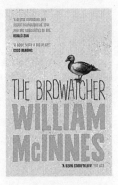

The Birdwatcher

This is a story about a bloke who's losing his hearing; a bird that can't fly but likes being read to; and a teenage daughter who doesn't know who to be angry at.

It's about a woman living with the echo of illness finding out how much fun it can be to trust someone; a man called Murph who has a secret; and Perry Como.

It's part love story, part Hot Diggity moments of discovery, whether they happen in a rainforest or while sitting on a verandah, or in somebody's heart.

Most of all, it's about giving yourself the gift to be still while you wait for the lights to change or the rain to stop, so you have time to think.

For all of us, there are memories and secrets that can change our lives. If we let them.

'I was left with a warm feeling in my belly' *Daily Telegraph*

'Memorable, heart-warming and brave' *West Australian*

ISBN 978 0 7336 3297 6

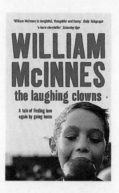

The Laughing Clowns

Peter Kennedy is remarkably happy with his life. Yet something is not quite right, and it started with a dream that smelt of luncheon meat.

When a developer asks Peter to assess a prime piece of Queensland real estate – the Pickersgill Peninsula Showgrounds – he jumps at the chance. It will give him time out from having to be with the family he loves. And it will take him back to his childhood home; to his parents, his twin sister, Pearl, and his brother, Gary, the TV weatherman.

Over these few days, he will come to realise that sometimes when you go back to where you came from you find out how much you actually have, and how much you could lose. He just has to make his mind up, and listen to the advice that's given by, of all people – the King of Hot Dogs.

But will he?

'McInnes generates warmth and humour' *Weekend Australian*

'skilfully constructed ... insightful, understated and very funny' *Sydney Morning Herald*

ISBN 978 0 7336 3027 9

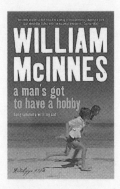

A Man's Got to Have a Hobby

'Life goes by so fast that sometimes it is good to wait and let the memories catch up. And there is no better place to do that than the backyard where you grew up.'

A Man's Got to Have a Hobby looks back at the life of Colin McInnes, father of five, handyman and habitual Stubbie wearer, and his wife Iris, lover of shopping-centre openings, Volkswagens and Dean Martin. It is a story about cane toads and backyard barbecues, French-Canadian Hell Drivers and footy games. Through the memories of their second son, William, we are transported to a time when incinerators took up space in every yard and K-Tel glass cutters were the pride of many a home.

This is a book about people who aren't famous, but should be. It's about love, hope and fear, laughter, death and life.

'a great Aussie yarn' *Sunday Mail*

'William McInnes compels with the sheer delightfulness of his memoir, and with his fine ability to spin a damn funny yarn.' *Sunday Telegraph*

ISBN 978 0 7336 2078 2

GET THE WHOLE STORY AT:

www.hachette.com.au

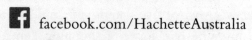

facebook.com/HachetteAustralia

twitter.com/HachetteAus